Weather and Climate Experiments

FACTS ON FILE
SCIENCE EXPERIMENTS

Weather and Climate Experiments

Pamela Walker
Elaine Wood

Facts On File
An imprint of Infobase Publishing

Weather and Climate Experiments

Text and artwork copyright © 2010 by Infobase Publishing

Editor: Frank K. Darmstadt
Copy Editor for A Good Thing, Inc.: Betsy Feist
Project Coordination: Aaron Richman
Art Director: Howard Petlack
Production: Victoria Kessler
Illustrations: Hadel Studios

Facts On File, Inc.
An imprint of Infobase Publishing
132 West 31st Street
New York NY 10001

Library of Congress Cataloging-in-Publication Data
Walker, Pam, 1958-
Weather and climate experiments / Pamela Walker, Elaine Wood.
p. cm.—(Facts on File science experiments)
Includes bibliographical references and index.
ISBN 978-0-8160-7808-0
1. Weather—Experiments. 2. Dynamic meteorology–Experiments. 3. Science–Study and teaching (Middle school–Activity programs. 4. Science–Study and teaching (Secondary) –Activity programs. I. Wood, Elaine, 1950- . Title.
QC981.W25 2010
551.5078–dc22
2009011504

Facts On File books are available at special discounts when purchased in bulk quantities for businesses, associations, institutions, or sales promotions. Please call our Special Sales Department in New York at 212/967-8800 or 800/322-8755.

You can find Facts On File on the World Wide Web at http://www.factsonfile.com

Printed in the United States of America

Bang AGT 10 9 8 7 6 5 4 3 2 1

This book is printed on acid-free paper.

Contents

Preface

For centuries, humans have studied and explored the natural world around them. The ever-growing body of knowledge resulting from these efforts is science. Information gained through science is passed from one generation to the next through an array of educational programs. One of the primary goals of every science education program is to help young people develop critical-thinking and problem-solving skills that they can use throughout their lives.

Science education is unique in academics in that it not only conveys facts and skills; it also cultivates curiosity and creativity. For this reason, science is an active process that cannot be fully conveyed by passive teaching techniques. The question for educators has always been, "What is the best way to teach science?" There is no simple answer to this question, but studies in education provide useful insights.

Research indicates that students need to be actively involved in science, learning it through experience. Science students are encouraged to go far beyond the textbook and to ask questions, consider novel ideas, form their own predictions, develop experiments or procedures, collect information, record results, analyze findings, and use a variety of resources to expand knowledge. In other words, students cannot just hear science; they must also do science.

"Doing" science means performing experiments. In the science curriculum, experiments play a number of educational roles. In some cases, hands-on activities serve as hooks to engage students and introduce new topics. For example, a discrepant event used as an introductory experiment encourages questions and inspires students to seek the answers behind their findings. Classroom investigations can also help expand information that was previously introduced or cement new knowledge. According to neuroscience, experiments and other types of hands-on learning help transfer new learning from short-term into long-term memory.

Facts On File Science Experiments is a six-volume set of experiments that helps engage students and enable them to "do" science. The high-interest experiments in these books put students' minds into gear and give them opportunities to become involved, to think independently, and to build on their own base of science knowledge.

As a resource, Facts On File Science Experiments provides teachers with new and innovative classroom investigations that are presented in a clear, easy-to-understand style. The areas of study in the six-volume set include forensic science, environmental science, computer research, physical science, weather and climate, and space and astronomy. Experiments are supported by colorful figures and line illustrations that help hold students' attention and explain information. All of the experiments in these books use multiple science process skills such as observing, measuring, classifying, analyzing, and predicting. In addition, some of the experiments require students to practice inquiry science by setting up and carrying out their own open-ended experiments.

Each volume of the set contains 20 new experiments as well as extensive safety guidelines, glossary, correlation to the National Science Education Standards, scope and sequence, and an annotated list of Internet resources. An introduction that presents background information begins each investigation to provide an overview of the topic. Every experiment also includes relevant specific safety tips along with materials list, procedure, analysis questions, explanation of the experiment, connections to real life, and an annotated further reading section for extended research.

Pam Walker and Elaine Wood, the authors of Facts On File Science Experiments, are sensitive to the needs of both science teachers and students. The writing team has more than 40 years of combined science teaching experience. Both are actively involved in planning and improving science curricula in their home state, Georgia, where Pam was the 2007 Teacher of the Year. Walker and Wood are master teachers who hold specialist degrees in science and science education. They are the authors of dozens of books for middle and high school science teachers and students.

Facts On File Science Experiments, by Walker and Wood, facilitates science instruction by making it easy for teachers to incorporate experimentation. During experiments, students reap benefits that are not available in other types of instruction. One of these benefits is the opportunity to take advantage of the learning provided by social interactions. Experiments are usually carried out in small groups, enabling students to brainstorm and learn from each other. The validity of group work as an effective learning tool is supported by research in neuroscience, which shows that the brain is a social organ and that communication and collaboration are activities that naturally enhance learning.

Experimentation addresses many different types of learning, including lateral thinking, multiple intelligences, and constructivism. In lateral thinking, students solve problems using nontraditional methods. Long-established, rigid procedures for problem-solving are replaced by original ideas from students. When encouraged to think laterally, students are more likely to come up with unique ideas that are not usually found in the traditional classroom. This type of thinking requires students to construct meaning from an activity and to think like scientists.

Another benefit of experimentation is that it accommodates students' multiple intelligences. According to the theory of multiple intelligences, students possess many different aptitudes, but in varying degrees. Some of these forms of intelligence include linguistic, musical, logical-mathematical, spatial, kinesthetic, intrapersonal, and interpersonal. Learning is more likely to be acquired and retained when more than one sense is involved. During an experiment, students of all intellectual types find roles in which they can excel.

Students in the science classroom become involved in active learning, constructing new ideas based on their current knowledge and their experimental findings. The constructivist theory of learning encourages students to discover principles for and by themselves. Through problem solving and independent thinking, students build on what they know, moving forward in a manner that makes learning real and lasting.

Active, experimental learning makes connections between newly acquired information and the real world, a world that includes jobs. In the 21st century, employers expect their employees to identify and solve problems for themselves. Therefore, today's students, workers of the near future, will be required to use higher-level thinking skills. Experience with science experiments provides potential workers with the ability and confidence to be problem solvers.

The goal of Walker and Wood in Facts On File Science Experiments is to provide experiments that hook and hold the interest of students, teach basic concepts of science, and help students develop their critical-thinking skills. When fully immersed in an experiment, students can experience those "Aha!" moments, the special times when new information merges with what is already known and understanding breaks through. On these occasions, real and lasting learning takes place. The authors hope that this set of books helps bring more "Aha" moments into every science class.

Acknowledgments

This book would not exist were it not for our editor, Frank K. Darmstadt, who conceived and directed the project. Frank supervised the material closely, editing and making invaluable comments along the way. Betsy Feist of A Good Thing, Inc., is responsible for transforming our raw material into a polished and grammatically correct manuscript that makes us proud.

Introduction

Few other fields of science are more intimately tied to our daily lives than those associated with the study of weather and climate. Our culture's interest in weather is reflected in the daily news, both print and electronic, that brings us up-to-the minute weather information. For many people, current weather information is essential in making daily plans. As a blend of all the events that occur in the atmosphere, weather includes precipitation and temperature. Since weather varies from day to day, and even hour to hour, updates enable us to plan activities and tell us whether to wear raincoats or sun visors to school and work.

Climate is not as variable as weather, but the two are intimately connected. Some families decide where they want to live based on the climate, and there are plenty of choices. From those who want hot, dry conditions to those who prefer cool, moist weather, there is something for everyone. Although different regions of the Earth experience different climates, the daily weather patterns within each climate are interconnected. Unusual weather in one region of the globe can spawn changes in weather on the far side of the globe.

Study of the weather and climate helps students understand weather conditions and the science behind weather research. Temperature, barometric pressure, wind, and precipitation are just a few of the types of data routinely collected and analyzed by meteorologists. In *Weather and Climate Experiments*, students are given opportunities to carry out hands-on activities using weather instruments similar to those of experts. Through experimentation, learners make hypotheses, collect and interpret data, draw conclusions, and share their information with others.

Weather and Climate Experiments is one book in a set titled Facts On File Science Experiments from Facts On File, Inc. The text contains 20 proven classroom experiments that broaden students' understandings of both science facts and the nature of science. Appropriate for both middle and high school classes, the investigations are enjoyable and interesting.

Activities in *Weather and Climate Experiments* include "The Heat-Retaining Properties of Water and Soil," in which students explore the effects of water's high heat capacity on temperatures. Worldwide weather phenomena are analyzed in "Modeling El Niño." In "Sources of Carbon Dioxide in the Air" and "Levels of Ultraviolet Radiation in Local Ecosystems" students analyze levels of two weather and climate factors that are impacted by human activities.

In "Variables That Affect Cloud Formation," students make "clouds" under varying circumstances and analyze their findings. "What Type of Hair Makes the Most Accurate Hygrometer?" examines the effectiveness of student-made hygrometers that resemble the earliest examples of these instruments. The science behind fascinating weather is revealed in two investigations, "How Are Snowflakes Formed?" and "How Do Tornadoes Form?" Students collect data over a period of days then analyze the data to draw conclusions in "Temperature and Barometric Pressure," "Does Sunset Color Vary With Weather Conditions?" and "Student-Constructed Weather Stations."

"How Does Topography Affect Flash Flooding?" looks at the causes of flash floods. "How Accurate Are Weather Predictions?" enables students to record and check the predictions of forecasters. Students reenact the work of early scientists in "A Custom Temperature Scale." "A Convection Box" shows students how temperature affects the movement of air masses. "Intensity of Insolation" explains the effects of the angle of the Sun's rays on the amount of heat transferred to Earth.

Although traditional laboratories are highly valued because they teach science skills, one of the most effective teaching techniques is inquiry learning. This practice pushes students to go beyond a set of directions and get involved in the problem-solving aspects of science. By carrying out inquiry labs, students have the opportunities to test their own ideas for solving problems. The experiment "Factors That Affect Evaporative Rates" asks students to set up an experiment comparing the effects of three factors on rate of evaporation. In "How Does Distance Affect Solar Energy Absorption?" students design and carry out an experiment to test the effect of distance on energy absorption.

Since relevance is one of the keys to learning, weather and climate are ideal topics for engaging learners in science. By studying weather, students can understand more about what is going on in the world around them. They can also learn to appreciate the work that scientists put into gathering weather data and making accurate predictions. *Weather and Climate Experiments* provides activities that enable students to understand more about the forces that affect their lives as well as how science works.

Safety Precautions

REVIEW BEFORE STARTING ANY EXPERIMENT

Each experiment includes special safety precautions that are relevant to that particular project. These do not include all the basic safety precautions that are necessary whenever you are working on a scientific experiment. For this reason, it is absolutely necessary that you read and remain mindful of the General Safety Precautions that follow. Experimental science can be dangerous and good laboratory procedure always includes following basic safety rules. Things can happen quickly while you are performing an experiment—for example, materials can spill, break, or even catch on fire. There will not be time after the fact to protect yourself. Always prepare for unexpected dangers by following the basic safety guidelines during the entire experiment, whether or not something seems dangerous to you at a given moment.

We have been quite sparing in prescribing safety precautions for the individual experiments. For one reason, we want you to take very seriously the safety precautions that are printed in this book. If you see it written here, you can be sure that it is here because it is absolutely critical.

Read the safety precautions here and at the beginning of each experiment before performing each lab activity. It is difficult to remember a long set of general rules. By rereading these general precautions every time you set up an experiment, you will be reminding yourself that lab safety is critically important. In addition, use your good judgment and pay close attention when performing potentially dangerous procedures. Just because the book does not say "Be careful with hot liquids" or "Don't cut yourself with a knife" does not mean that you can be careless when boiling water or using a knife to punch holes in plastic bottles. Notes in the text are special precautions to which you must pay special attention.

GENERAL SAFETY PRECAUTIONS

Accidents can be caused by carelessness, haste, or insufficient knowledge. By practicing safety procedures and being alert while conducting experiments, you can avoid taking an unnecessary risk. Be sure to check the individual experiments in this book for additional safety regulations and adult supervision requirements. If you will be working in a laboratory, do not work alone. When you are working off site, keep in groups with a minimum of three students per group, and follow school rules and state legal requirements for the number of supervisors required. Ask an adult supervisor with basic training in first aid to carry a small first-aid kit. Make sure everyone knows where this person will be during the experiment.

PREPARING

- Clear all surfaces before beginning experiments.
- Read the entire experiment before you start.
- Know the hazards of the experiments and anticipate dangers.

PROTECTING YOURSELF

- Follow the directions step by step.
- Perform only one experiment at a time.
- Locate exits, fire blanket and extinguisher, master gas and electricity shut-offs, eyewash, and first-aid kit.
- Make sure there is adequate ventilation.
- Do not participate in horseplay.
- Do not wear open-toed shoes.
- Keep floor and workspace neat, clean, and dry.
- Clean up spills immediately.
- If glassware breaks, do not clean it up by yourself; ask for teacher assistance.
- Tie back long hair.
- Never eat, drink, or smoke in the laboratory or workspace.
- Do not eat or drink any substances tested unless expressly permitted to do so by a knowledgeable adult.

USING EQUIPMENT WITH CARE

- Set up apparatus far from the edge of the desk.
- Use knives or other sharp, pointed instruments with care.

- Pull plugs, not cords, when removing electrical plugs.
- Clean glassware before and after use.
- Check glassware for scratches, cracks, and sharp edges.
- Let your teacher know about broken glassware immediately.
- Do not use reflected sunlight to illuminate your microscope.
- Do not touch metal conductors.
- Take care when working with any form of electricity.
- Use alcohol-filled thermometers, not mercury-filled thermometers.

USING CHEMICALS

- Never taste or inhale chemicals.
- Label all bottles and apparatus containing chemicals.
- Read labels carefully.
- Avoid chemical contact with skin and eyes (wear safety glasses or goggles, lab apron, and gloves).
- Do not touch chemical solutions.
- Wash hands before and after using solutions.
- Wipe up spills thoroughly.

HEATING SUBSTANCES

- Wear safety glasses or goggles, apron, and gloves when heating materials.
- Keep your face away from test tubes and beakers.
- When heating substances in a test tube, avoid pointing the top of the test tube toward other people.
- Use test tubes, beakers, and other glassware made of Pyrex™ glass.
- Never leave apparatus unattended.
- Use safety tongs and heat-resistant gloves.
- If your laboratory does not have heatproof workbenches, put your Bunsen burner on a heatproof mat before lighting it.
- Take care when lighting your Bunsen burner; light it with the airhole closed and use a Bunsen burner lighter rather than wooden matches.

- Turn off hot plates, Bunsen burners, and gas when you are done.
- Keep flammable substances away from flames and other sources of heat.
- Have a fire extinguisher on hand.

FINISHING UP

- Thoroughly clean your work area and any glassware used.
- Wash your hands.
- Be careful not to return chemicals or contaminated reagents to the wrong containers.
- Do not dispose of materials in the sink unless instructed to do so.
- Clean up all residues and put in proper containers for disposal.
- Dispose of all chemicals according to all local, state, and federal laws.

BE SAFETY CONSCIOUS AT ALL TIMES!

1. The Heat-Retaining Properties of Water and Soil

Topic

Water has the ability to retain heat longer than soil.

Introduction

Have you ever stepped outside on a cold morning to find the ground beneath you frozen solid? Even so, the water in a nearby large body of water may still be in the liquid state. How can soil freeze while water in a big lake or in the ocean remains in the liquid state? The answer is found in water's unusual chemical properties.

Water is a *polar molecule*, so it has a slight positive charge on one end and a slight negative charge on the other end (see Figure 1). Like tiny magnets, the negative end of one water molecule is attracted to the positive end of another. These attractive forces between water molecules are called *hydrogen bonds*. In this experiment, you will see how the hydrogen bonds in water affect its ability to hold heat.

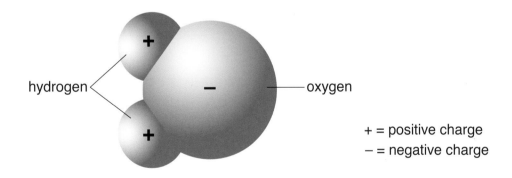

hydrogen

oxygen

+ = positive charge
− = negative charge

Figure 1
Water molecule

Time Required

55 minutes

Materials

- ◦◦ 2 large Styrofoam™ cups
- ◦◦ 2 thermometers
- ◦◦ heat lamp
- ◦◦ graduated cylinder
- ◦◦ soil (about 1 cup)
- ◦◦ water (about 1 cup)
- ◦◦ electronic scale or triple-beam balance
- ◦◦ clock or timer
- ◦◦ marking pen or labels
- ◦◦ science notebook

Safety Note Take special care when working with the heat lamp. Please review and follow the safety guidelines at the beginning of this volume.

Procedure

1. Half fill a Styrofoam™ cup with soil.
2. Determine the mass of the soil. To do so:
    a. Place the empty cup on the electronic scale and find its mass. Record the mass in your science notebook.
    b. Remove the empty cup and replace it with the cup of soil.
    c. Determine the mass of the cup of soil and record it in your science notebook.
    d. Subtract the mass of the empty cup from the mass of the cup and soil to find the mass of the soil.
3. Place an equal mass of water in the empty cup. (Remember that 1 milliliter [ml] of water has a mass of 1 gram [g].)
4. Gently insert a thermometer into each cup.
5. Place both cups under the heat lamp and leave them there for 30 minutes (min).

6. While the cups of water and soil are under the heat lamp, copy the data table in your science notebook and answer Analysis questions 1 and 2.

7. After 30 min, turn off the heat lamp. Read the temperature on each thermometer. On your data table in the row titled "Starting temperature," record the temperatures of the soil and water.

8. Every 2 min for the next 20 min, check the temperature in each cup. Record the temperatures on the data table in the appropriate row.

9. Answer Analysis questions 3 through 9.

Data Table		
	Cup of soil	**Cup of water**
Starting temperature		
2 minutes		
4 minutes		
6 minutes		
8 minutes		
10 minutes		
12 minutes		
14 minutes		
16 minutes		
18 minutes		
20 minutes		

Analysis

1. Write a hypothesis that explains why the first freeze of winter may cause ice crystals to form in the soil, but does not cause water in a large lake to freeze. Explain the logic behind your hypothesis.

2. Why do you think it is important to use the same mass of soil and water in this experiment?

3. In your experiment, which showed the greatest change in temperature, the soil or water?

4. According to your experimental results, which substance can hold heat the longest, soil or water?

5. How did your experimental findings compare to your hypothesis?

6. Chicago, Illinois, is on the banks of Lake Michigan. In Chicago, the temperature may be 14 degrees Fahrenheit [°F] (– 10 degrees Celsius [°C]) for a week, yet Lake Michigan does not freeze. Using your experimental results, explain why.

7. Based on your experimental results, how do you think the difference in the heat-retaining abilities of soil and water might affect climate along the coast?

What's Going On?

Water can retain heat longer than most other substances. The ability of a substance to hold heat without becoming very warm itself is referred to as *heat capacity*. Heat energy is measured in calories. Heat energy of 1 calorie is required to raise the temperature of 1 g of water 1°C. In comparison, only one-eighth as much energy is needed to raise the temperature of 1 g of iron by the same amount. Water has any unusually high heat capacity due to the presence of hydrogen bonds between adjacent water molecules.

For most substances, heat directly affects molecules, causing them to vibrate faster and move apart. Water reacts differently to heat. When water is heated, the initial input of energy breaks apart the hydrogen bonds between water molecules. During this period, water maintains its temperature. After all the hydrogen bonds are broken, individual water molecules begin to vibrate and separate, and the temperature increases. Therefore, it takes more heat to raise the temperature of 1 g of water than it does for any other substance. The reverse is also true; as water cools, the water molecules first form hydrogen bonds with each other, maintaining their temperature as they do so. Eventually, cooling slows the motion of the water molecules and the temperature of a water sample drops. The presence of hydrogen bonds causes water to heat slower, and cool slower, than other substances.

Connections

The ability of water to hold heat affects climate. Because water holds heat better than soil, ocean temperatures show little variation at night, remaining relatively warm. On nearby land masses, temperatures may drop significantly. When ocean-warmed air rises at night, cool air from the land flows in to replace it, causing wind to blow offshore. During the day, the land warms up faster than the ocean, reversing the situation. Warm air over land rises and cooler ocean air flows in to replace it. For this reason, onshore winds blow during the day.

Water's heat-retaining abilities mean that cities located along coastlines experience less-drastic changes in temperature from day to night than inland regions. In addition, the climates of these regions are milder, showing fewer temperature extremes. For example, the average high temperature in coastal San Francisco during the summer is 68°F (20°C); 20 miles (32.19 kilometers [km]) inland, the average high is 87°F (31°C). Although climate is a complex phenomenon, part of this difference is due to the fact that the ocean does not heat as quickly in the summer as the nearby land. As a result, areas near the ocean are cooler than areas that are surrounded by land.

 ### Want to Know More?

See appendix for Our Findings.

Further Reading

The Biology Project. Biochemistry, "The Chemistry of Water." Department of Biochemistry and Molecular Biophysics, University of Arizona, January 28, 2003. Available online. URL: http://www.biology.arizona.edu/ biochemistry/tutorials/chemistry/main.html. Accessed August 9, 2008. The Biology Project provides excellent tutorials in all areas of science, including the polarity of water molecules.

Carpi, Anthony. "Water, Properties and Behavior," VisionLearning, 2003. Available online. URL: http://www.visionlearning.com/library/module_ viewer.php?mid=57. Accessed August 9, 2008. In this tutorial, the author explains how hydrogen bonding affects water's behavior.

Poon, Alvar S. C., and Henry Yam. Physics CUMK, "Large Specific Heat Capacity of Water," 2002. Available online. URL: http://www.hk-phy.org/ contextual/heat/tep/temch/island_e.html. Accessed August 12, 2008. This interactive Web site shows how soil and water heat at different rates.

2. Student-Constructed Weather Stations

Topic

Homemade weather instruments can be used to monitor local conditions.

Introduction

Have you ever listened to the weather report on your local news and wondered where all of that information came from? How can *meteorologists* collect data on temperature, rainfall, and wind direction and speed and use it to predict weather conditions? The information needed for making accurate forecasts comes from weather stations located around the world.

A weather station is made up of several different instruments that can collect data about the weather conditions. Most weather stations contain a thermometer to measure temperature, a *rain gauge* to find how much rain fell, a wind vane to tell the direction of the wind, an *anemometer* to find wind speed, and a *barometer* to determine atmospheric pressure. Instruments in weather stations may be monitored manually once a day or by computers every hour. Except for the rain gauge and *wind vane*, instruments are usually stored in a small, vented box.

The first weather station in the United States was established by Thomas Jefferson (1743–1826). Because he was intensely interested in nature, Jefferson created a station at his home in Virginia some time before 1776, when he made his first weather diary entry. His accurate measurements and continuous records have provided most of what we know about weather in early America. Jefferson recorded much of the same kind of information that weather stations log today. In this experiment, you will construct a weather station and use it to monitor weather conditions.

 Time Required

45 minutes on day 1
15 minutes a day for two follow-up days

Materials

- large weatherproof plastic storage container or wooden box
- outdoor thermometer
- tape
- clear, cylinder-shaped jar (like an olive jar)
- funnel
- ruler
- permanent marker
- 6 plastic drinking straws
- card stock (about the size of a 3-by-5-inch index card)
- scissors
- 2 straight pins
- 2 pencils with erasers
- modeling clay
- compass
- 4 small paper drinking cups
- stopwatch (or watch with a second hand)
- stapler
- glass jar with a wide neck (like a baby food jar)
- balloon
- rubber band
- glue
- paper (one sheet)
- string (a few feet)
- science notebook

Safety Note   Please review and follow the safety guidelines at the beginning of this volume.

Procedure, Day 1

1. Tape an outdoor thermometer to the bottom of the inside of large weatherproof box. Turn the box on its side, so that the thermometer is at the back of the box. This box will serve as your weather station.

2. Create a rain gauge from a clear, cylinder-shaped jar. Hold a ruler against the outside of the jar so that the edge of the ruler lines up with the bottom of the jar. Use a permanent marker to mark the jar every one-eighth of an inch (in.) (0.3 centimeters [cm]). Label your markings. Place a funnel in the top of the jar and secure with tape (see Figure 1).

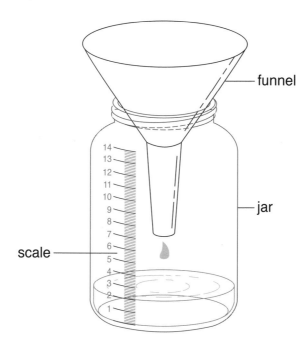

Figure 1

3. Build a wind vane. To do so:

   a. Draw and cut out the point of a small arrow (about 1 in. [2.5 cm] long) from card stock. Draw and cut out the tail of an arrow (about the same size) from card stock.

   b. Use scissors to make slits in each end of a drinking straw. Place the arrow point into the slits at one end of the straw. Secure with tape. Place the arrow tail on the other end of the straw and secure with tape.

   c. Push a straight pin through the center of the straw. Place the point of the straight pin into the eraser of a pencil (see Figure 2).

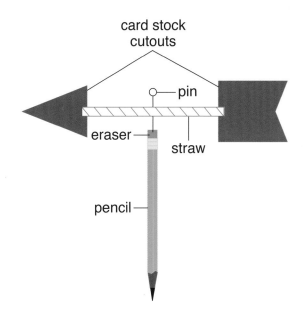

Figure 2

4. Construct an anemometer. To do so:

   a. Arrange four drinking straws so that they form a cross. Secure them at the center with tape.

   b. Staple a small paper drinking cup to the end of each straw so that all of the cups open toward the same direction.

   c. Make an X on one cup with a permanent marker (to make counting rotations easier).

   d. Push a straight pin through the center of the cross that was made by the four straws. Place the point of the pin into the eraser of a pencil (see Figure 3).

5. Create a barometer. To do so:

   a. Out of the balloon, cut a circle that is large enough to cover the mouth of a wide-necked jar (like a baby food jar).

   b. Tightly stretch the balloon cutout over the top of the jar and secure it with a rubber band.

   c. Place a dot of glue in the center of the balloon cutout.

   d. Lay a plastic drinking straw so that one end is glued to the center of the balloon and the other end hangs over the edge of the jar (see Figure 4).

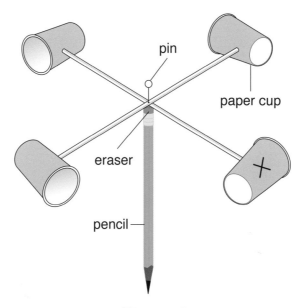

Figure 3

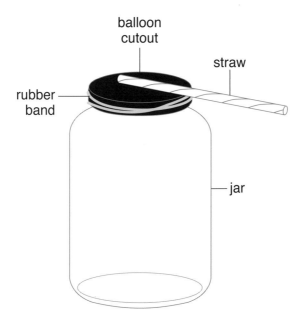

Figure 4

6. Take all of your equipment for collecting weather data outside to a secure location selected by your teacher. Set up the station. To do so:

   a. Stand the box on its side. Place the rain gauge on top of the box. Use modeling clay or tape to secure the jar in place.

   b. Use modeling clay or tape to mount the pencil of the weather vane to the top of the weather station.

   c. Use modeling clay or tape to secure the anemometer to the weather station.

     d. Tape a sheet of paper to one inside wall of the weather station box. Place the barometer in front of the paper. Using a ruler, draw a line even with the top of the jar. Write "High Pressure" above the line and "Low Pressure" below it. Mark the initial position of the straw on the paper.

7. Collect information about outdoor conditions from each instrument in your weather station. For each instrument, record your findings on the data table. To collect data:

     a. Read the temperature on the thermometer.

     b. Observe the position of the needle of the barometer and record whether the air pressure is high ("rising") or low ("falling").

     c. Determine the amount of rainfall by measuring the water that collects in the rain gauge. (On the first day, you will not have any rain in the rain gauge unless you are setting up your station during a shower.)

     d. Use a compass to determine which direction the wind vane is pointing.

     e. Determine the speed of the wind by counting how many times the anemometer turns in 1 minute (min).

     f. Record your findings on the data table

Procedure, Follow-up Days

1. Repeat step 7 for 2 days.

Data Table			
	Day 1	**Day 2**	**Day 3**
Temperature (°F)			
Rainfall			
Wind direction			
Wind speed (turns per minute)			
Air pressure			

Analysis

1. Watch the weather report on the local news or go online to get the weather report for your city on the same days that you collected data with your weather station. How does the data compare?

2. What are some reasons your data may be different from the meteorologist's report?

3. How does air pressure relate to the weather conditions?

4. Why do you think it is necessary to measure wind direction?

5. How do you think temperature affects the other factors that influence weather (such as air pressure, wind, and precipitation)?

6. What factors, other than the data that could be collected from this weather station, are important to consider when describing the weather?

What's Going On?

The weather patterns here on Earth ultimately begin with the Sun. The Sun's rays heat the Earth, which causes the temperature to rise. Because the Earth is tilted on its axis, the Sun heats the Earth unevenly. Regions near the equator are heated more than those at the poles. Additionally, landmasses absorb more heat than bodies of water. Variations in temperature caused by the uneven heating cause differences in air pressure and humidity across the globe.

Warm air tends to be lighter and have less pressure than cold air. Because of this, warm air generally moves on top of cooler air. This movement creates wind coming from the direction of the high-pressure front. If there is a large pressure difference where two fronts meet, the wind will blow faster. Also, as two pressure fronts meet, the movement of air upward creates clouds which, in turn cause precipitation.

Connections

Have you ever looked at the sky on a hot, humid day to see huge thunderheads forming? These are known as *cumulonimbus clouds*, and they are formed when warm, moist air cools very quickly. When air cools, it causes the water vapor in the air to condense into water, forming a cloud. As the water condenses, energy is released, causing the air to be warmer than it was originally. As a result, the air continues to rise. This rising air creates the tall, towering clouds commonly known as thunderheads. Once the cloud can no longer hold water droplets, the condensed water falls to the Earth as rain or hail.

As more and more water condenses within a cumulonimbus cloud, water droplets, hail, and ice crystals contained within the cloud collide. These collisions build up electrical charges. The positive and negative charges tend to separate to different regions of the cloud. The negative charges are generally concentrated near the bottom of the cloud, while the positive charges are usually near the upper regions of the cloud. The ground also tends to be concentrated with positive charges. Once the difference in charge becomes great enough, there is often a transfer of electrical energy that we see as *lightning*. Lightning strikes generally occur between two regions of a cloud or between a cloud and the ground. Lightning strikes are very dangerous because they can be five times hotter than the surface of the Sun.

Want to Know More?

See appendix for Our Findings.

Further Reading

National Oceanic and Atmospheric Administration. "Weather." Available online. URL: http://www.noaa.gov/wx.html. Accessed August 10, 2008. NOAA provides data and information on all types of weather conditions around the world.

National Weather Service, Climate Prediction Center. "Short-Term Forecasts," August 7, 2008. Available online. URL: http://www.cpc.ncep. noaa.gov/. Accessed August 10, 2008. On this Web site, you may view weather forecasts for the next few days or for the next month.

Weather Bug, 2007. Available online. URL: http://weather.weatherbug. com/. Accessed August 10, 2008. The Weather Bug provides up-to-date weather data on a national and regional basis.

3. How Are Snowflakes Formed?

Topic

The unique structures of snowflakes can be observed in a chamber that produces ice crystals.

Introduction

You may have heard that no two snowflakes are alike. Since we cannot view every snowflake that has ever formed, no one knows for sure if this is true. But we do know that there is an almost infinite number of possibilities for snowflake structure. Regardless of the unique structure that snowflakes take, they are always six-sided. The hexagonal shape of every snowflake is due to the structure of water molecules (see Figure 1). To maintain their stability when they form ice, water molecules arrange themselves into six-sided structures held together by *hydrogen bonds*. Every snowflake begins as a single tiny ice crystal inside a cloud. As water condenses onto the original crystal, each side grows into the intricate patterns that you can see when you examine a snowflake.

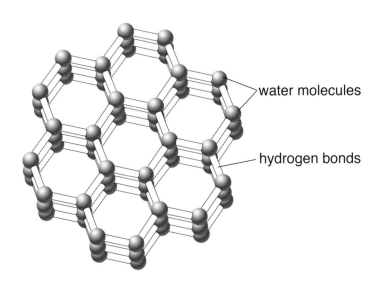

water molecules

hydrogen bonds

Figure 1
Molecular structure of water

The clouds we see in the sky year-round are mostly made up of tiny ice crystals like those that form snowflakes. The temperature and conditions within the cloud determine whether or not the tiny ice crystals will develop into snowflakes. The temperature range within the cloud determines the basic shape of a snowflake, and then the snowflake continues to form as it falls to Earth. The atmospheric conditions through which a snowflake travels determine the way ice crystallizes and the shape that the snowflake will have when it reaches the Earth. In this experiment, you will build a snow chamber and observe the formation of a snowflake.

Time Required

60 minutes

Materials

- crushed dry ice
- gloves
- empty 20-ounce (oz) plastic bottle with cap
- 3 Styrofoam™ cups, 32-oz size
- scissors
- kitchen sponge
- 4 straight pins
- thin fishing line (1 pound test)
- paper clip
- tape
- water (about 1 cup)
- paper towels
- magnifying glass
- pencil or pen
- science notebook

> **Safety Note**   Use gloves when handling dry ice, as it can cause tissue damage if it comes in contact with bare skin. Use caution when working with scissors and straight pins. Please review and follow the safety guidelines at the beginning of this volume.

Procedure

1. Using the cap of the 20-oz plastic bottle as a guide, cut a hole in the bottom of one Styrofoam™ cup so that the bottle cap can be inverted and fit snugly into the hole. Refer to Figure 2.

2. Stack the cup with the cap in it inside of the two other Styrofoam™ cups.

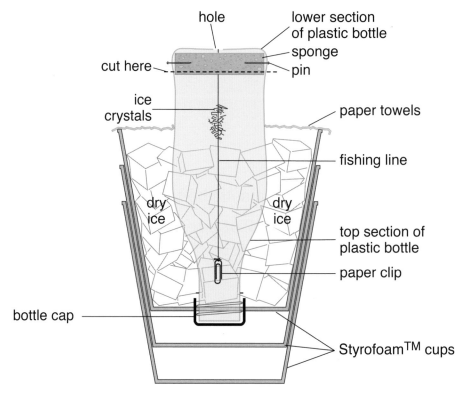

Figure 2

3. Using scissors, cut around the plastic bottle about one inch (in.) (2.5 centimeters [cm]) from the bottom to remove the lower portion of the bottle.

4. Cut a slit or a small hole in the center of the lower section of the bottle.

5. Cut a kitchen sponge into a circular shape so that it fits into the lower section of the bottle. Make a small hole in the center of the sponge. (This hole will line up with the hole in the lower section of the bottle once the sponge is put in place.)

6. Place the sponge circle in the lower section of the bottle. Push four straight pins through the plastic bottle and into the sponge in order to hold it securely in place.

7. Cut a piece of fishing line so that it is about 1 in. (2.5 cm) shorter than the height of the entire bottle.

8. Tie the fishing line to a paper clip. Thread the paper clip end of the fishing line through the holes in the lower section of the bottle and the sponge. Secure the other end of the fishing line to the outside of the bottle with tape.

9. Invert the top section of the plastic bottle into the nested Styrofoam™ cups.

10. Wet the kitchen sponge with tap water, then place the lower section with the sponge onto the inverted apparatus. Attach the two parts of the bottle with tape. The paper clip should swing freely inside of the bottle; adjust the fishing line length if necessary.

11. Fill the top Styrofoam™ cup with dry ice so that it surrounds the entire bottle. Cover the dry ice with paper towels and secure to the bottle and cup with tape.

12. Observe the fishing line inside the bottle. Ice crystals should begin to form after about 5 minutes (min), and there should be large crystals after 45 min to an hour.

13. Be sure to refill the Styrofoam™ cup with dry ice as it gets low.

14. Observe the ice crystals with a magnifying glass. Record your observations in your science notebook.

Analysis

1. Draw a sketch of the ice crystals that formed within your chamber.

2. Did your crystals look like snowflakes? Why or why not?

3. How was the formation of these ice crystals similar to the formation of an actual snowflake? How was it different?

4. Was it necessary for the sponge in the base of the bottle to be wet? What would have happened if it had been dry?

4. Modeling El Niño

Topic

The effects of El Niño on world climate can be demonstrated.

Introduction

El Niño is a phenomenon that occurs when the typical Pacific *trade winds* slow down, causing drastic weather changes across the globe. The change in weather conditions occurs around the time of Christmas off the coast of South America, so it is named *El Niño* or "little boy," referring to the Christ child. Scientists are not exactly sure why the change in wind patterns occurs, but it happens periodically every 2 to 7 years. The winds tend to pick back up after a year, but weather patterns can be affected in some areas of the globe for up to 5 years.

In normal, non-El Niño conditions, trade winds blow across the Pacific from the east to the west. The winds push warm surface water toward the western Pacific, causing an *upwelling* of cool water from deeper in the ocean in the eastern Pacific. The cool water from deep in the ocean is nutrient-rich, and it makes the eastern Pacific highly productive during this time. However, during El Niño, the trade winds relax and no upwelling occurs. In this experiment, you will create a model to explain the cause of El Niño.

Time Required

25 minutes

Materials

- large clear plastic container (18 inches [in.] by 4 in. by 4 in. [45.7 centimeters (cm) by 10.2 cm by 10.2 cm] works well)
- 1 to 1.5 cups of mineral oil or baby oil

➠   bottle of blue food coloring

➠   oil-based red paint (about 1 teaspoon)

➠   large mixing bowl

➠   paint stirring stick or large spoon

➠   funnel

➠   hair dryer

➠   2 index cards

➠   tape

➠   pencil or pen

➠   access to water

➠   science notebook

Safety Note   Use caution when using electrical appliances near water. Please review and follow the safety guidelines at the beginning of this volume.

Procedure

1. Fill the plastic container so that it is about two-thirds full of water.

2. Add enough food coloring to the water to produce a rich, blue color.

3. Pour the oil into a bowl. Add a few drops of red paint and mix well with a stirring stick or spoon until the color is evenly distributed.

4. Pour the red paint gently through the funnel into the plastic container so that it makes a layer on top of the water. This represents the warm and cool layers of water within the Pacific Ocean.

5. Label the right side of the container "East" and the left side "West."

6. Turn on the hair dryer and blow it into the "East" end of the container (toward the west). Record your observations in your science notebook.

7. Turn off the hair dryer. Observe what happens to the liquids in the container and record your observations in your science notebook.

Analysis

1. What happened to the liquids in the container while the hair dryer was blowing on them? What ocean condition does this represent?

2. What happened when the hair dryer stopped blowing across the water? What ocean condition does this represent?

3. How are ocean temperatures related to weather?

4. What type of weather patterns could be expected in the eastern Pacific during El Niño? In the western Pacific?

5. How might El Niño affect marine life and wildlife around the Pacific?

What's Going On?

The trade winds that normally blow westward over the Pacific Ocean push warm water toward the landmasses in the western Pacific. This causes the sea surface to be about 1.6 feet (ft) (0.5 meters [m]) higher on the coast of Asia than it is on the coast of South America. The movement of warm surface water away from the eastern Pacific causes an upwelling of deep ocean water and brings nutrients and microscopic organisms closer to the surface. As a result, marine organisms as well as birds and other wildlife have plenty of food. However, during El Niño, warm water is pushed toward South America, creating a decline in the food available to ocean organisms. Therefore, fish and other organisms must migrate to find food or they die.

The normal Pacific trade winds are responsible for the development of *precipitation* that moves toward Asia, Australia, and Indonesia. This is because water evaporates more readily from warm water then from cool water. The evaporated water forms clouds, which creates precipitation that the trade winds carry to the western Pacific. However, as the warm water shifts eastward during El Niño, the precipitation shifts along with it (see Figure 1), causing flooding in North and South America and drought in Australia, Asia, and Indonesia. Of course, the shifts in weather patterns affect more than just the continents around the Pacific Ocean. Wind patterns are global, so a change in warm air currents in the Pacific displaces wind patterns in other locations, causing global weather changes.

Normal conditions

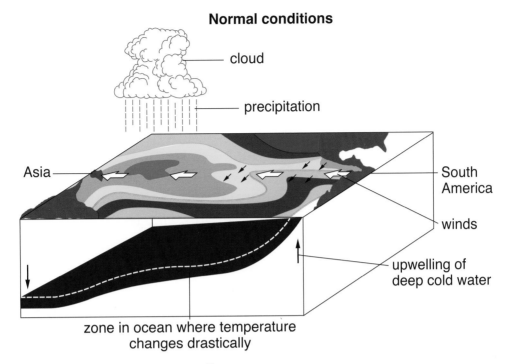

El Niño conditions

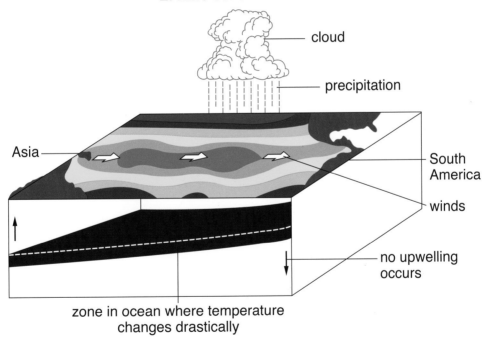

Figure 1

Connections

Sometimes conditions do not return to normal immediately after El Niño. Often, but not always, El Niño is followed by another trend of climatic changes caused by a phenomenon known as *La Niña*. Once El Niño has dissipated, the normal, westward trade winds that blow over the Pacific return, but they often blow harder than normal. As a result, water temperatures in the Pacific drop because the warm surface water is being pushed away by the strong trade winds. Because of this, the water temperatures are much lower than normal near Asia (see Figure 2).

La Niña, which means "the little girl," was so named because it has the opposite effects of those brought on by El Niño, "the little boy." La Niña tends to cause flooding in Australia, Asia, and Indonesia and drought in North and South America. La Niña events, while not as well known as El Niño, can have equally drastic worldwide climate effects. The low ocean temperatures of La Niña generally last 9 to 12 months, but can persist for up to 2 years. Both El Niño and La Niña are part of what is known as the *El Niño–Southern Oscillation*, or ENSO. Although these events occur irregularly and cannot be predicted, they are occurring more frequently in recent years, which some scientists suggest may be attributed to global warming.

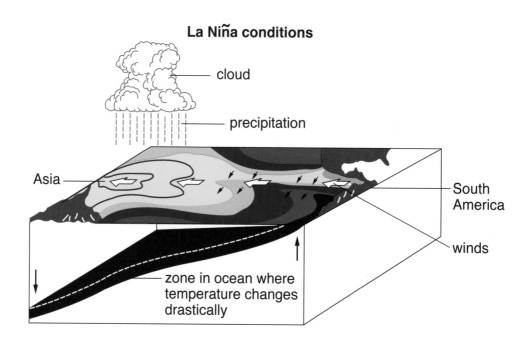

Figure 2

Want to Know More?

See appendix for Our Findings.

Further Reading

NASA. "El Niño," January 22, 2003. Available online. URL: http://kids. earth.nasa.gov/archive/niño/intro.html. Accessed December 22, 2008. This Web page provides a simple yet accurate description of El Niño.

The National Academies. "El Niño and La Niña: Tracing the Dance of Ocean and Atmosphere," 2007. Available online. URL: http://www7. nationalacademies.org/opus/elNiño.html. Accessed December 22, 2008. This Web site give a detailed explanation of changes in global weather due to El Niño.

National Oceanic and Atmospheric Administration. "What Is an El Niño?"Available online. URL: http://www.pmel.noaa.gov/tao/elnino/el-nino-story.html. Accessed August 10, 2008. This NOAA Web site explains the science behind El Niño.

5. Factors That Affect Evaporative Rates

Topic

The rate at which water evaporates from surfaces varies depending on weather conditions.

Introduction

Have you ever seen a big puddle just after a rain shower and found that it was gone the next day? Most likely, the puddle evaporated. *Evaporation* is the change of state from liquid to a gas. Evaporation is occurring when you see steam rising from a pot of boiling water; the liquid water is becoming water vapor, a gas. Evaporation can occur quickly when water boils because the water molecules are absorbing so much energy from the stove that they can no longer exist in a liquid state and must spread out as a gas. However, you do not have to boil water for evaporation to occur. It happens all the time in nature.

Water exists in three different states, solid (ice), liquid (water), and gas (water vapor or steam). Water is constantly changing states depending on the atmospheric conditions such as temperature and pressure. Water falls to the ground as *precipitation,* and then evaporates into the air where it later condenses into clouds of water and ice so that it can produce more precipitation. This natural series of events is known as the *water cycle*. In this activity, you will explore some factors that can affect the rate of evaporation.

Time Required

90 minutes

Materials

- glass aquarium
- large cardboard box

26

- 4 beakers, 400 milliliters [ml]
- 4 beakers, 600 ml
- 4 aluminum pie plates
- hot plate
- thermometer
- ruler
- triple-beam balance or electronic scale
- 100-ml graduated cylinder
- ice
- salt
- fan
- misting sprayer
- heat lamp
- pencil or pen
- access to water
- science notebook

Safety Note   Use caution if using glassware, the hot plate, heat lamp, and any electrical devices, especially around water. Please review and follow the safety guidelines at the beginning of this volume.

Procedure

1. Your job is to design and perform an experiment comparing three factors that affect the rate at which water evaporates. Some factors you may want to test are temperature, wind, humidity, surface area, and amount of sunlight.

2. You can use any of the supplies provided by your teacher, but you will not need to use all of them.

3. Keep in mind that each experiment you set up needs a *control,* a part of the experiment that is not changed in any way. For example, if you place water in a beaker and put the beaker under a heat lamp

to find out how heat affects rate of evaporation, you will need to set up an identical beaker of water that you do not put under the heat lamp as your control.

4. Before you conduct your experiment, decide exactly what you are going to do. Write the steps you plan to take (your experimental procedure) and the materials you plan to use (materials list) on the data table. Show your procedure and materials list to the teacher. If you get teacher approval, proceed with your experiment. If not, modify your work and show it to your teacher again.

5. Once you have teacher approval, assemble the materials you need and begin your procedure.

6. Collect your results on a data table of your own design.

Analysis

1. What factors did you choose to compare in your experiment? Why did you choose those?

2. Which of the factors tested in your experiment sped up evaporation the most? Which affected the rate of evaporation the least?

3. Based on your findings from this experiment, what weather conditions might cause the most evaporation from bodies of water?

4. The rain that falls in your area originally evaporated from some area, formed clouds, then produced precipitation. Where do you think this rain may have evaporated from to form your local rain clouds and rain? Explain your reasoning.

5. Describe the steps you took to ensure that your experiment was a controlled experiment. Why is it important in an experiment to keep all factors the same, other than the one you are testing?

What's Going On?

The rate of water evaporation depends on several factors. Warm water evaporates faster than cool water. This is because heat is a type of energy, and energy causes the water particles to move fast. The faster particles move, the more likely they are to spread out from a liquid state into a gaseous state. The amount of surface area of a body of water also has an impact over the evaporation rate. A wide, shallow pond will evaporate much faster than a small, very deep pond holding the same amount of water. Water must come in contact with air in order to evaporate, and if there is more water exposed to air, more of it can turn into a gas.

Data Table	
Your experimental procedure	
Your materials list	
Teacher's approval	

The evaporation of water not only depends on the condition of the water, but also the condition of the air around it. The *humidity* of the air above a body of water affects the evaporation rate of that water. Dry air above a body of water has the ability to absorb more water vapor than moist air. If there is a lot of humidity, the air cannot hold as much water because it already has a high concentration of water vapor. Windy conditions also tend to speed up evaporation because if air is moving quickly, there is more air flowing over a body of water. As air moves over the water, it absorbs water vapor, so the more air flow, the more evaporation.

Connections

Have you ever seen someone put salt into a pot before they boil water? Have you ever wondered why they do that? Adding salt to water can actually cause the boiling temperature to rise, which can essentially make your food cook faster in the boiling water. This phenomenon is known as *boiling point elevation*. Water typically boils at 212 degrees Fahrenheit [°F] (100 degrees Celcius [°C]). When water boils, it is evaporating to form water vapor. In its pure liquid state, water cannot get any hotter than 212°F (100°C) without turning into vapor. As long as that pot of water boils, regardless of how much you turn up the heat, it will not get any hotter. However if you add a substance like salt to the water, it allows the temperature to get hotter than 212°F (100°C).

Adding substances to water can cause boiling point elevation because the particles actually get in the way of the water leaving its liquid state to form vapor. Because the evaporation of water depends on water molecules reaching the surface to become a gas, other particles mixed in with the water decrease the number of water molecules that reach the surface. Consequently, the water absorbs more heat and the temperature rises so that the water molecules can overcome the obstacle of decreased surface area due to a foreign substance. The more particles that are added, the more the temperature will rise to enable the water to evaporate. Since table salt is an *ionic compound* made up of two atoms, sodium and chlorine, it actually breaks up into two particles when placed in water, increasing the boiling point elevation even more.

 Want to Know More?

See appendix for Our Findings.

Further Reading

Grow. "Evaporation." Available online. URL: http://www.grow.arizona.edu/Grow--GrowResources.php?ResourceId=208. Accessed October 14, 2008. This Web site maintained by the Geotechnical, Rock and Water Resource Library explains evaporation using excellent graphics.

U.S. Geological Survey. "The Water Cycle." Available online. URL: http://ga.water.usgs.gov/edu/watercycle.html. Accessed October 14, 2008. The USGS provides detailed information on how water travels through the environment.

Weather and Climate. "Evaporation and Condensation." Available online. URL: http://www.ace.mmu.ac.uk/Resources/Teaching_Packs/Key_Stage_4/Weather_Climate/04.html. Accessed August 10, 2008. Accurate, student-friendly information on evaporation of water is presented on this Web site.

6. Sources of Carbon Dioxide in the Air

Topic

The amount of carbon dioxide in samples of gas can be compared.

Introduction

The climate on Earth has changed many times throughout history. In the past, alterations in the Earth's orbit and extended periods of volcanic activity have caused alternating episodes of warming and cooling. In the past 200 years, human activity has led to an overall rise in Earth's average temperature, an occurrence known as *global warming*, due to the increased production of *greenhouse gases* (see Figure 1).

Rays of sunlight entering the Earth's atmosphere warm the planet's surface. The Earth absorbs a portion of these rays, while some are reflected back into space. Greenhouse gases in Earth's atmosphere

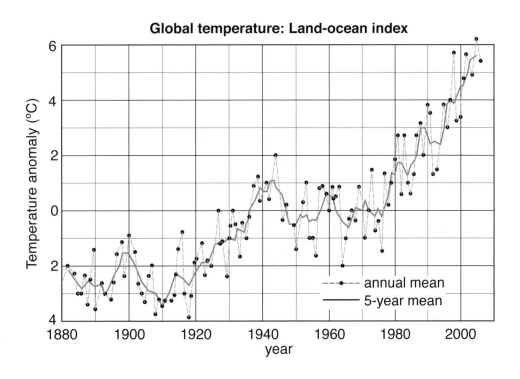

Figure 1

act as a layer of insulation, keeping some of the reflected heat from escaping into space. In this way, the greenhouse gases, which include carbon dioxide and methane, keep the planet warm enough to support life. However, abnormal thickening of the layer of greenhouse gases has caused an unusual amount of warming. As a result, the Earth's temperature has risen higher than in the past. In this experiment, you will compare the amount of carbon dioxide in samples of gas.

Time Required

45 minutes

Materials

- 4 large test tubes
- test-tube rack
- 4 balloons
- 4 twist ties
- graduated cylinder
- funnel (glass or metal)
- leather work gloves
- rubber hose (that will fit the end of the funnel)
- straw
- modeling clay (a marble-size piece)
- bromthymol blue indicator in a dropper bottle
- dilute ammonia solution (1 part ammonia to 50 parts distilled water) in a dropper bottle
- 100 milliliters (ml) vinegar
- 60 ml distilled water
- 5 grams (g) baking soda
- Erlenmeyer flask
- bicycle pump
- labeling tape

- marker
- graph paper
- access to an automobile
- science notebook

Safety Note   **Wear goggles at all times during this experiment. Do not collect gases from the automobile exhaust; your teacher will do it for you. Be careful when working with glassware and chemicals. Please review and follow the safety guidelines at the beginning of this volume.**

Procedure

1. Label your test tubes A, B, C, and Control. Fill each test tube with 15 ml of distilled water and 10 drops of bromthymol blue indicator.

2. Label the four balloons as A, B, C, and Control.

3. When filling the balloons with air from different sources, keep these points in mind:

   a. Each balloon should be tied off with a twist tie, not tied into a knot.

   b. Each balloon should be filled to the same diameter (about 7 to 8 inches [in] [17 to 20 centimeter (cm)]).

4. Fill balloon A with your breath. Blow into the balloon in order to inflate it to the appropriate size. Seal with a twist tie.

5. Ask your teacher to fill balloon B with car exhaust. To do so, your teacher will:

   a. Attach rubber hosing to the neck of the funnel.

   b. Attach a balloon to the other end of the rubber hose.

   c. While wearing thick gloves, hold the funnel up to the exhaust pipe of an idling vehicle until the balloon is inflated to the appropriate size.

   d. Seal with a twist tie.

6. Fill balloon C with an almost pure sample of carbon dioxide. Place 100 ml of vinegar into an Erlenmeyer flask. Add about 5 g of baking soda to the flask, and immediately put a balloon over the neck of the flask. Seal with a twist tie when the balloon has inflated to the appropriate size.

7. Fill the Control balloon with atmospheric air. Use a bicycle pump to inflate the balloon to the appropriate size. Seal with a twist tie.

8. Wrap one end of a straw with modeling clay, making a funnel-shaped collar that the neck of the balloon will fit into. Place the neck of balloon A onto the clay collar and hold it in place to ensure that no air leaks out. Place the other end of the straw into test tube A. Remove the twist tie and squeeze the balloon gently until all of the air bubbles through the solution in the test tube. Record the color of the solution on the data table. Repeat with balloons and tubes B, C, and Control.

9. Notice the color in each test tube. When carbon dioxide is bubbled through water, it creates carbonic acid, which causes the bromthymol blue to turn yellow. In the test tubes that showed a change in color, add dilute ammonia, one drop at a time, until the carbonic acid is neutralized and the liquid turns the same color as that in the control tube. Record the number of drops needed for each test tube on the data table.

Data Table		
Sample	Test tube color	Number of drops of ammonia
A		
B		
C		
Control		0

Analysis

1. Plot your results on a bar graph with each air sample on the X-axis and the number of drops of ammonia on the Y-axis.

2. Which air sample contained the most carbon dioxide? Which one had the least?

3. Scientists have stated that automobile exhaust is one of the largest contributors to the amount of carbon dioxide in the atmosphere. Do your results validate this point? Why or why not?

4. What could be done to decrease the amount of carbon dioxide released by automobiles in the United States?

5. What are some other sources of carbon dioxide gas in the atmosphere? How could the carbon dioxide from these sources be reduced (or eliminated)?

6. What are some ways that you personally can reduce the amount of greenhouse gases that you release?

What's Going On?

The term *greenhouse gas* refers to any of the gases that blanket the Earth's atmosphere and help to trap heat near its surface. Greenhouse gases are primarily water vapor and carbon dioxide, but include methane, ozone, nitrous oxide, *chlorofluorocarbons (CFCs)*, and many other trace gases. The emission of all greenhouse gases has increased drastically with industrialization, which began in the 1800s. The majority of greenhouse gases are due to the burning of fossil fuels, such as coal and petroleum (which is used to make gasoline).

Since industrialization began, people have become increasingly dependent on fossil fuels as a source of energy and means of transportation. Consequently, the emission of carbon dioxide continues to increase drastically over time (see Figure 2). The problem of increased levels of carbon dioxide in the atmosphere is compounded by *deforestation*. Because the number of plants available to take up carbon dioxide for photosynthesis continues to drop, the gas lingers in the air and becomes part of the blanket of gases that trap heat near Earth. The emission of greenhouse gases will continue to increase in the future unless fossil fuel combustion is dramatically decreased. Unfortunately, no fuel sources have been discovered that prove to be as effective and reliable as coal and petroleum.

Connections

The recorded average temperature on Earth has increased by about 1.3 degrees Fahrenheit (°F) (0.74 degrees Celsius [°C]) in the past 100 years. This may seem like only a slight warming, but it is significant and directly impacts weather patterns and the abundance of species on Earth. Many organisms are very sensitive to temperature changes. One such organism is coral. A change in water temperature of just 1°C (1.8°F) can cause *coral bleaching* and death. Corals are critically important in the ocean community. They constantly clean ocean water by filter feeding. In addition, coral reefs provide a barrier to many landmasses, and they are a vital source of protection for marine species. The majority of the fish in the ocean were hatched in coral reefs, so without these important organisms, there would be a drastic decline in fish populations.

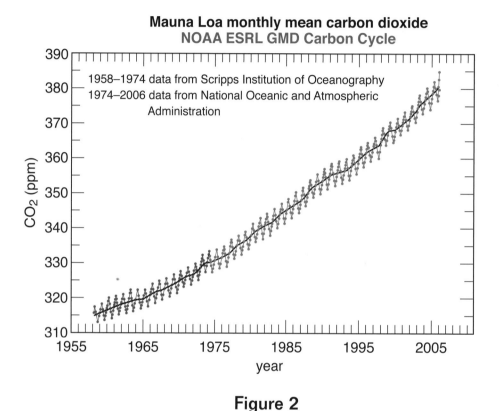

Mauna Loa monthly mean carbon dioxide
NOAA ESRL GMD Carbon Cycle

1958–1974 data from Scripps Institution of Oceanography
1974–2006 data from National Oceanic and Atmospheric Administration

Figure 2

Global warming can also cause an increase in the amount of severe weather around the world. As ocean temperatures rise, even slightly, their heat energy provides fuel for developing storms by increasing the rate of water evaporation. Strong hurricanes and typhoons capable of massive destruction have resulted from these warmer-than-usual waters. In addition to powerful storms, warm ocean currents melt polar ice caps, increasing the volume of water in the oceans, which leads to destructive tidal waves and floods. Where global warming is concerned, a slight increase in temperature is significant.

Want to Know More?

See appendix for Our Findings.

Further Reading

Energy Information Administration. "Greenhouse Gases, Climate Change, and Energy," May, 2008. Available online. URL: http://www.eia.doe.gov/bookshelf/brochures/greenhouse/Chapter1.htm. Accessed August 17, 2008. The U.S. Department of Energy provides an excellent description of the problems caused by greenhouse gases and global warming.

Parish, Zakia D. "Greenhouse Gases: The Chemistry Behind the Culprits," 2007. Available online. URL: http://www.yale.edu/ynhti/curriculum/units/2007/4/07.04.05.x.html. Accessed February 7, 2009. Parish describes characteristics of the atmosphere, identifies greenhouse gases, describes their properties, and discusses their effects on Earth's climates.

Thompson, Andrea. "Charge: Carbon Dioxide Hogs Global Warming Stage," March 29, 2007. Available online. URL: http://www.livescience.com/environment/070329_non_co2.html. Accessed August 17, 2008. Thompson discusses the culprits of global warming and some of the problems they cause.

7. Levels of Ultraviolet Radiation in Local Ecosystems

Topic

Levels of ultraviolet radiation in two neighboring ecosystems can be measured and compared.

Introduction

Ultraviolet (UV) radiation, a type of energy wave that is emitted by the Sun, is one of several types of energy that make up the *electromagnetic spectrum*. Other electromagnetic rays include radio waves, microwaves, infrared rays, visible light, X-rays, and gamma rays (see Figure 1). The distinguishing factor among all types of electromagnetic radiation is the amount of energy contained in the wave, a quantity indicated by its *wavelength*. UV light has a shorter wavelength than visible light, meaning that UV rays carry more energy than the typical sunlight that enables us to see.

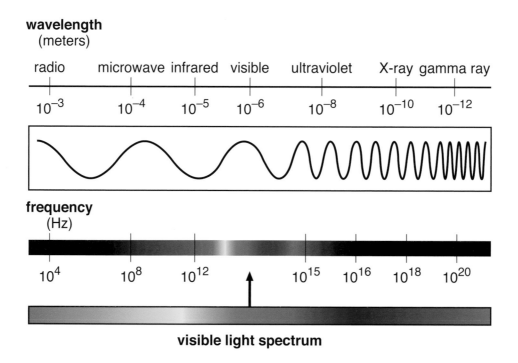

Figure 1

The electromagnetic spectrum

UV radiation is present in three different bands: *UVA, UVB,* and *UVC.*
UVC bands are absorbed by the upper atmosphere and do not reach the
Earth's surface. However, UVA and UVB rays are a concern to humans
because of their ability to cause sunburn and skin damage. Humans can
prevent this damage by using broad-spectrum Sun blocks and sunscreens.
However, these rays do not damage only humans. Many other organisms
are affected by UV radiation and may be harmed by high levels of UV light.
In this activity, you will design an experiment to compare the level of UV
radiation present in two neighboring ecosystems.

Time Required

60 minutes (time may vary depending on experiment design)

Materials

- 2 UV sensors (electronic or indicator cards)
- stopwatch
- altimeter
- outdoor thermometer
- measuring tape
- pencil or pen
- science notebook

Safety Note Please review and follow the safety guidelines at the
beginning of this volume.

Procedure

1. Your job is to design and perform an experiment to compare the
   levels of UV radiation in two neighboring ecosystems.
2. You can use any of the supplies provided by your teacher, but you
   will not need to use all of them.
3. Before you conduct your experiment, decide exactly what you are
   going to do. Write the steps you plan to take (your experimental
   procedure) and the materials you plan to use (materials list) on the

data table. Show your procedure and materials list to the teacher. If you get teacher approval, proceed with your experiment. If not, modify your work and show it to your teacher again.

4. Once you have teacher approval, assemble the materials you need and begin your procedure.

5. Collect your results on a data table of your own design.

Data Table	
Your experimental procedure	
Your materials list	
Teacher's approval	

Analysis

1. Describe the two ecosystems you chose for your experiment. Why did you choose these particular locations?

2. Explain the steps you took to ensure that your experiment was performed under controlled circumstances. Why is this important?

3. How did the UV radiation compare in the two locations?

4. What factors within the ecosystem might influence the level of UV radiation that was measured?

5. How might the organisms in your tested areas be affected by the UV radiation present?

6. What type of ecosystem do you think would have higher levels of UV radiation than the ones you observed? Why?

What's Going On?

Of the three types of UV radiation, the only two that actually reach the Earth's surface are UVA and UVB rays. UVB rays have a longer wavelength and therefore carry less energy than the stronger UVA rays. UVB rays tend to cause sunburn in humans because the uppermost layer of skin absorbs them. UVA rays, since they are more powerful, penetrate deeper into the skin and cause wrinkling, loss of elasticity, and premature aging. Both types of UV radiation are capable of causing skin cancer in humans. Aside from their effects on the human population, UV radiation can also have damaging effects on many other organisms within an ecosystem. Higher levels of UV light can cause damage to plants and photosynthetic algae, including marine *plankton*. Since these organisms are at the base of the *food web* in their ecosystems, the effects of UV radiation can be widespread.

The amount of UV light that reaches the surface of the Earth varies from place to place. Areas closer to the equator experience more sunlight than those at the north and south poles, therefore the UV light is more intense. Additionally, more UV light reaches the ground at higher altitudes—since the ground is higher, UV radiation does not have a chance to dissipate before reaching the surface. Cloud cover and smog can also affect the amount of UV radiation in an area because they absorb the rays before they reach the lower atmosphere. Locations near major cities tend to experience less UV damage than those in remote locations. Smog in cities, which is bad for the respiratory system, has a high level of *ozone* in it, which absorbs damaging UV rays. Exposure to UV radiation also varies based on whether the majority of organisms are found out in the open or under tree cover, or if they are near a body of water or on sand or snow, which can reflect and ultimately intensify UV rays.

Connections

The Earth's atmosphere absorbs 97 to 99 percent of all UV radiation. However, the small amount that actually reaches the ground can have serious effects on organisms. A small oxygen molecule known as ozone found in the upper atmosphere is responsible for absorbing the damaging UV light that is radiated by the Sun. However, in the mid-1970s, scientists discovered that the layer of ozone that protected the Earth was thinning, and in 1985 a large hole in the ozone layer was discovered over Antarctica. The depletion of the ozone layer is blamed on the use of *chlorofluorocarbons (CFCs)*, which were widely employed in aerosol cans and as a refrigerant in air conditioners. CFCs were banned in most countries in the late 1980s, but the damage to the ozone layer remains.

Because of ozone depletion, more UV radiation reaches the surface of the Earth now than in the past. This has been especially problematic in areas in the Southern Hemisphere near the Antarctic ozone hole, such as Australia and New Zealand. The increase in UV radiation has led to an increased number of cases of skin cancer, including *basal* and *squamous cell carcinomas* and *malignant melanoma*, as well as an increased number of individuals with *cataracts*. In addition to these effects on humans, increased UV radiation causes damage to marine ecosystems by reducing the abundance of plankton, a major food source in ocean food webs, which is very sensitive to UV light. Many plants are also undergoing damage from harmful UV rays, especially crops that depend on a *symbiotic relationship* with *cyanobacteria* as a source of nitrogen. Cyanobacteria are also extremely sensitive to UV levels, and if they cannot survive, crops suffer.

 Want to Know More?

See appendix for Our Findings.

Further Reading

Allen, Jeannie. "Ultraviolet Radiation: How It Affects Life on Earth," NASA, September 6, 2001. Available online. URL: http://earthobservatory.nasa.gov/Library/UVB/. Accessed August 23, 2008. Allen discusses effects of UV radiation on the biosphere.

Environmental Protection Agency, SunWise Program. "UV Radiation," January 3, 2008. Available online. URL: http://www.epa.gov/sunwise/uvradiation.html. Accessed August 23, 2008. The EPA explains the types of UV radiation and problems caused by each type.

NASA. "Visible Earth. TOMS: Ultraviolet Radiation Exposure," June 8, 2006. Available online. URL: http://visibleearth.nasa.gov/view_rec.php?id=1520. Accessed August 23, 2008. NASA graphically shows levels of UV radiation on the Earth using a Total Ozone Mapping Spectrometer.

8. Variables That Affect Cloud Formation

Topic

A cloud chamber can help identify the variables that affect the process of cloud formation.

Introduction

What makes up a cloud? Children may believe that clouds are made of the fluffy cotton balls they resemble. However, clouds are actually condensed droplets of water and ice crystals that form when warm air cools. Warm, damp air can rise to high altitudes where it comes in contact with cooler air. Cooling causes the water vapor to condense onto tiny particles of dust known as *condensation nuclei*. These droplets of water suspended in the sky form clouds.

Clouds come in many shapes and sizes, and they can evaporate and vanish just as quickly as they form. The shapes of clouds are ultimately determined by the temperature and pressure in the atmosphere. When clouds become so large that they can no longer hold all of the water vapor condensed in them, the water leaves the cloud and falls to the ground as *precipitation*. In this experiment, you will build a cloud-generating chamber and determine the variables that affect cloud formation.

Time Required

45 minutes

Materials

- large glass jar with lid
- graduated cylinder
- 200-milliliter (ml) beaker
- hot plate
- ice (3 or 4 cubes)

- water
- matches
- hot hands or an oven mitt
- science notebook

Safety Note   Use caution when using hot plate, glassware, and matches. Please review and follow the safety guidelines at the beginning of this volume.

Procedure

1. Pour about 100 ml water into a beaker. Place the beaker on a hot plate and heat until it is boiling.

2. Use hot hands (or an oven mitt) to remove the beaker from the heat. Remove the lid from the jar and pour hot water into the jar.

3. Turn the jar lid upside down so that it makes a shallow dish. Place the ice cubes into the lid. (See Figure 1.)

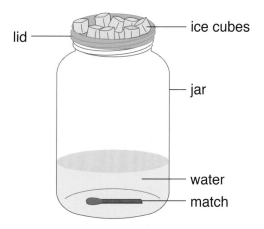

Figure 1

4. Strike a match so that it burns for a few seconds and then blow it out. Place the match into the jar with the hot water.

5. Place the lid containing ice cubes onto the mouth of the jar.

6. Record your observations in your science notebook.

7. Repeat the procedure, except use tap water instead of boiling water in the jar. Record your observations.

Analysis

1.   Sketch and describe the appearance of the cloud you created.

2.   Why was ice placed in the inverted lid of the jar? What would happen if no ice were added?

3.   What was the purpose of the match in the container?

4.   Which experiment created better clouds: the one with boiling water or the one using tap water? Why do you think this is so?

5.   Why do you think most of the clouds on Earth form over the ocean?

6.   Clouds form due to decreasing temperatures as well as increasing pressure. Design a cloud chamber that creates clouds because of changes in pressure instead of temperature.

What's Going On?

Water exists as solid, liquid, and gas, depending on the temperature and pressure. At the lowest temperatures and highest pressures, water exists as a solid, ice. In intermediate conditions, water exists as a liquid. At high temperatures and low pressures, water is a vapor. Because of this, warm air contains more water vapor than cooler air. Therefore, as warm air comes in contact with cool temperatures or high pressure, the water vapor within it condenses into its liquid form. However, water cannot simply condense in thin air. It must condense onto a substance such as a tiny dust speck or soot particle released from smoke. This is what causes a cloud to form.

Because of the uneven heating of the Earth's surface, the atmosphere contains bands of warm, high-pressure air and cool, low-pressure air. When the wind blows, it causes these bands to collide, resulting in clouds and weather systems. Such collisions happen quite a bit over the ocean because of the high rate of *evaporation* over bodies of water. After the warm, saturated air comes in contact with a cold front, *condensation* takes place. Additionally, clouds can form due to winds blowing over changing altitudes, such as mountain ranges. As air is forced upward by mountains, it comes in contact with cooler air higher in the atmosphere, forming clouds.

Connections

Geographic formations on Earth's surface often have a big influence on the weather patterns occurring over a landmass. When cold wind blows over the surface of lakes, clouds can form and precipitation can occur on the opposite side of the lake from which the wind was blowing. Additionally, as warm air passes over mountain ranges or areas of high elevation, clouds form that produce precipitation on the side of the mountain from which the wind was blowing. This effect can even shape the ecosystems that appear in the areas surrounding mountain ranges.

The shift of air upward over a mountain range causes precipitation to fall on the same side of the mountain from which the wind was blowing, known as the windward side. For instance, if the prevailing winds are blowing from the west, precipitation will generally fall on the western side of a mountain range or on top of the mountain. This creates what is known as the *rain shadow effect* on the opposite side of the mountain. Therefore, deserts tend to be found on one side of a mountain range but the ecosystem on the opposite side usually has much more vegetation (see Figure 2). An example of the rain shadow effect can be seen in Death Valley, the driest area on Earth, which lies east of the Sierra Nevada and the Pacific Coast ranges of Southern California. The rain shadow effect causes clouds to form and rain to fall on the western side of the mountains, but rain scarcely falls to the east.

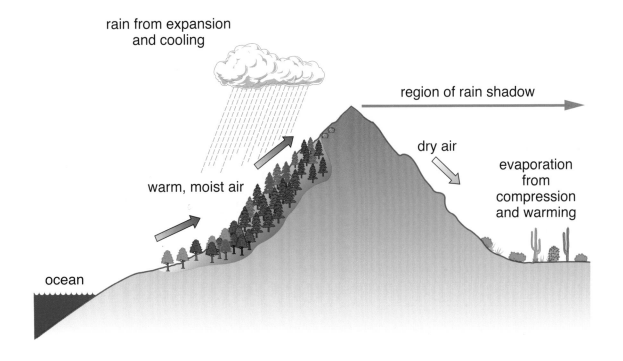

Figure 2

Want to Know More?

See appendix for Our Findings.

Further Reading

Hatheway, Becca. "How Clouds Form," Windows to the Universe, June 17, 2008. Available online. URL: http://www.windows.ucar.edu/tour/link=/ earth/Atmosphere/clouds/cloud_formation.html. Accessed August 23, 2008. This Web site offers a great explanation on how clouds form and links to other topics related to Earth science.

Met Office. "Clouds." Available online. URL: http://www.metoffice.gov.uk/ education/secondary/teachers/clouds.html. Accessed August 23, 2008. The effects of topography on cloud formation and other topics related to clouds are presented on this Web site.

WeatherQuestions.com. "How Do Clouds Form?" 2007. Available online. URL: http://www.weatherquestions.com/How_do_clouds_form.htm. Accessed August 23, 2008. This Web site features some great graphics to help explain cloud formation.

9. What Type of Hair Makes the Most Accurate Hygrometer?

Topic

Hygrometers using some types of hair are more accurate than those using other types.

Introduction

Have you ever been outside on a hot day just after it rained, when the air seems thick? The "thickness" you can feel in the air is *humidity*. A humidity reading describes the amount of water vapor in the air. Warm air can hold more water vapor than cool air because the air molecules are spread farther apart and contain extra space for water vapor to occupy. Measuring the amount of humidity in the air is a very important part of meteorology that helps predict weather patterns and determine the chance of precipitation.

Humidity is measured using an instrument called a *hygrometer*. The earliest hygrometers were made from strands of human hair. They were so accurate that an electronic hygrometer was not created until the 1960s. In this experiment, you will test different types of hair in hair hygrometers to determine which one is the most accurate.

Time Required

60 minutes on day 1
15 minutes over a 24-hour period

Materials

- 3 long (about 8 to 10 inches [in.] [20 to 25 centimeters (cm)]) strands of untreated human hair

- 3 long (about 8 to 10 in. [20 to 25 cm]) strands of permed human hair

- 3 long (about 8 to 10 in. [20 to 25 cm]) strands of highlighted human hair

- 3 pieces of flat Styrofoam™ or corrugated cardboard (about 4 in. by 9 in. [10 cm by 25 cm])

- 3 pushpins

- 3 dimes

- 3 flat pieces of plastic cut from a milk jug (about 3 in. by 4 in. [8 cm by 10 cm])

- tape

- scissors

- ruler

- hair dryer

- 20 percent rubbing alcohol solution (one part alcohol to four parts water)

- 3 cotton balls

- plastic container with lid (large enough to hold three hygrometers)

- 2 sponges

- warm water

- electronic hygrometer or a local weather report

- science notebook

Safety Note   Please review and follow the safety guidelines at the beginning of this volume.

Procedure

1. You will be making three hygrometers in this experiment. For each hygrometer, you will need three strands of the same type of hair. Using a cotton ball, wipe all the hairs with the 20 percent rubbing alcohol solution and allow them to dry. Make sure that all hairs are trimmed to the same length.

2. Answer Analysis Question 1.

3. First, prepare the hygrometer bases:

a. The cardboard or Styrofoam™ will act as a base. Place the base so that it stands lengthwise. If the material is too thin to stand on its own, you may need to use two pieces of Styrofoam™ glued together.

b. Cut two slits near the top of the base, about 1/4 in. apart (see Figure 2).

c. Repeat for the other two bases, cutting the slits in the same location on all bases.

4. To create a pointer for each hygrometer:

a. Cut a piece of thin plastic (like the plastic from a milk jug) to create an isosceles triangle that is about 2 in. (6 cm) wide at the base and 4 in. (10 cm) long.

b. Tape a dime into the center of the triangle near the tip (see Figure 1).

c. Cut two slits into one of the triangle sides about one quarter in. apart.

d. Repeat for the other two pointers. Make sure that all are the same size and shape and have the slits and dimes arranged in the same place.

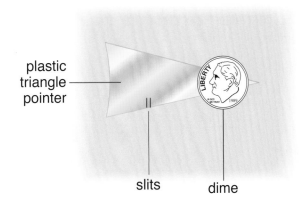

Figure 1

5. Assemble the hygrometers:

a. Take the three strands of hair (all the same type), hold them together and stretch them slightly to form a straight strand. Loop the hairs though the two slits in the top of the base. Tape them in place.

b. Arrange the pointer so that the slits are on the bottom of the triangle. Loop the free ends of the hair strands through the slits and tape them in place.

c. Position the pointer on the base so that the hair is stretched taut. Secure the pointer to the base using a pushpin placed through the center of the widest side of the triangle. The pointer should line up horizontally. (See Figure 2.)

d. Repeat for the other two hygrometers, making sure that all of them are assembled in the same way.

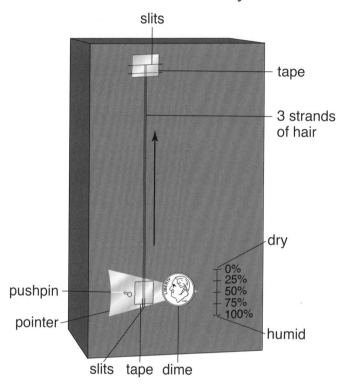

Figure 2

6. Calibrate the hygrometers:

    a. Place the hygrometers into a plastic container. Wet two sponges with warm water and place them in the bottom of the container. Close the lid of the container and leave the hygrometers for 30 minutes. (Alternatively, hygrometers can be placed in a closed room with a hot shower running). Mark the position of the pointer on each hygrometer base. Label it as "100 percent."

    b. Dry the hairs on each hygrometer with a hair dryer for 3 minutes. Mark the position of the pointer on the base of the hygrometer and label it so that it is pointing to "0 percent."

c. With a ruler, measure the distance between the 0 and 100 marks. Make a 50 percent mark exactly halfway between the 0 and 100 marks. Then, further divide the scale to read 25 percent (halfway between 0 and 50) and 75 percent (halfway between 50 and 100). The scale can be further divided if you wish.

7. Perform a test. To do so:

   a. Place all three hygrometers in the same general area so that they will experience the same conditions.

   b. Leave the hygrometers for at least 1 hour before taking the first humidity reading. Take two more readings over the next 24 hours.

   c. Each time you take a humidity reading, compare the measured humidity of each hygrometer with the reading from an electronic hygrometer or local weather report.

Data Table			
Type of hygrometer	Reading 1 time: _____	Reading 2 time: _____	Reading 3 time: _____
Untreated hair			
Permed hair			
Highlighted hair			
Electronic reading			

Analysis

1. Write a hypothesis as to which type of hair will be the most accurate in a hair hygrometer. Justify why you think this will be the case.

2. Why do human hairs show changes in high humidity?

3. Which way did the pointer move when it was more humid? Why do you think that it moved in that direction?

4. How did your measured results compare to the actual humidity?

5. Which type of hair made the most accurate hygrometer? Why do you think this is?

6. Was your hypothesis correct? If not, explain why.

7. How did your hygrometer readings change throughout the day? Why do you think this occurred?

What's Going On?

The amount of water vapor contained in the air can change throughout the day, depending on the weather conditions. Cold air tends to be drier, and as the temperature rises during the day, the humidity also tends to rise. Humidity can also predict the occurrence of precipitation. Before it rains, the humidity rises because of the excess moisture in the air. When it is raining, the humidity is 100 percent.

In order to understand why hair can be used in a hygrometer, it is necessary to know a little about the structure of hair. Human hair is made up of dead cells that are reinforced with the protein *keratin*. This is the same protein that hardens fingernails, bird beaks, and rhinoceros horns. Keratin is made up of amino acids, which attach to each other through several cross-linked bonds. They are also held together by weaker *hydrogen bonds*, which can be disrupted by water molecules. When water vapor is present in the air, water molecules are absorbed by the hair shaft, causing it to lengthen. In 100 percent humidity, hair increases in length by 2.5 percent. Chemically treated hair tends to increase in length more than untreated hair because of an increased number of breaks between the keratin bonds.

Connections

In the summer, humidity causes it to feel hotter than it actually is outside. The large amount of water vapor contained in the air decreases the amount of perspiration that can evaporate off of the body. Normally, the evaporation of sweat from the skin's surface causes a cooling effect because water must absorb some heat from the body to become vapor. However, if there is a lot of water vapor already present in the air, sweat cannot evaporate and people feel hot and sticky.

To account for the perceived difference in temperature due to humidity, *meteorologists* use a measure called the *heat index*. The heat index uses the temperature and relative humidity to determine how hot it feels outside in a shaded area. The temperature may even feel hotter when exposed to intense sunlight. The heat index is an important factor to take into consideration before spending time outdoors in warm weather. Without the cooling effect of perspiration, people can easily overheat, dehydrate, and experience *hyperthermia*, otherwise known as heat exhaustion or heat stroke.

Want to Know More?

See appendix for Our Findings.

Further Reading

HowStuffWorks. "What Is Relative Humidity and How Does it Affect How I Feel Outside," 2008. Available online. URL: http://science.howstuffworks. com/question651.htm. Accessed August 24, 2008. This Web site offers a simple and concise explanation of humidity.

Oblack, Rachelle. "How Does a Hygrometer Work." About.com Weather, 2008. Available online. URL: http://weather.about.com/od/ weatherinstruments/a/hygrometers.htm. Accessed August 24, 2008. The mechanics of hygrometers, both standard and hair, are described.

USA Today. "Understanding Humidity," 2008. Available online. URL: http:// www.usatoday.com/weather/whumdef.htm. Accessed September 15, 2008. This Web site includes a good glossary of terms related to relative humidity.

10. How Does Distance Affect Solar Energy Absorption?

Topic

Distance from the light source affects the amount of light energy absorbed by soil.

Introduction

The Sun is a hot star that serves as the primary source of energy for all life on Earth. Even though the Earth is about 93 million miles (150 million kilometers [km]) from the Sun, rays of light from the Sun are very intense and can be dangerous. Fortunately for Earth's inhabitants, the majority of the sunlight that travels to Earth from the Sun is either absorbed by the atmosphere or reflected back into space. The small amount of sunlight that passes through the atmosphere is used to warm the planet's surface.

Because of variations in Earth's surface in composition, altitude, and latitude, the planet does not absorb the Sun's rays evenly. Landmasses take in more of the Sun's energy than do bodies of water, and places near the equator receive more sunlight than those near the north and south poles. Additionally, the type of soil, the amount of vegetation in the soil, and the altitude of the ground that is receiving the sunlight affect energy absorption. In this activity, you will design an experiment to determine how its distance from the light source affects the amount of light energy absorbed by the soil.

Time Required

45 minutes

Materials

- 3 Styrofoam™ cups
- ring stand
- ring stand clamp

- triple-beam scale or electronic balance
- spoon
- heat lamp
- thermometer
- stopwatch or clock with a second hand
- meterstick
- bag of soil
- access to water
- science notebook

Safety Note   Use caution when using electrical appliances. Please review and follow the safety guidelines at the beginning of this volume.

Procedure

1. Your job is to design and perform an experiment to find out how the distance of soil from a light source affects the amount of energy it absorbs.

2. You can use any of the supplies provided by your teacher, but you will not need to use all of them.

3. Before you conduct your experiment, decide exactly what you are going to do. Write the steps you plan to take (your experimental procedure) and the materials you plan to use (materials list) on the data table on page 58. Show your procedure and materials list to the teacher. If you get teacher approval, proceed with your experiment. If not, modify your work and show it to your teacher again.

4. Once you have teacher approval, assemble the materials you need and begin your procedure.

5. Collect your results on a data table of your own design.

Analysis

1. Why is it important to keep all factors in an experiment controlled, or constant, except for the one that you are testing?

2. Describe the factors that you controlled during this experiment.

Data Table

Your experimental procedure	
Your materials list	
Teacher's approval	

3. Which of the soil samples tested absorbed the most energy? How did you determine this?

4. How does the distance of a soil sample from a light source affect the amount of energy it absorbs?

5. Explain why you think you got the results you did in this experiment.

6. Describe how the information you obtained from this experiment relates to varying temperatures on Earth.

What's Going On?

Sunlight is a form of *electromagnetic radiation*, energy that has electric and magnetic properties. The Sun's energy provides not only light, but also heat to warm Earth's surface and energy for processes such as *photosynthesis* that provide food to all organisms within an ecological *food chain*. Even though only a fraction of the light emitted from the Sun reaches the Earth, the energy provided by the Sun is essential to life on this planet.

The Earth's atmosphere prevents some of the Sun's energy from ever reaching the surface. Waves of sunlight are either scattered or absorbed as they hit particles in the upper atmosphere. Light that gets through the upper atmosphere is described as "transmitted" energy. This light continues to travel toward Earth where it may be *diffracted* by molecules in the air. The farther that sunlight has to travel, the better chance it has of being diffracted so it is carrying less energy by the time it reaches the planet's surface. This means that areas of lower elevation and areas that are farther from direct sunlight, such as those at the poles, receive less energy from the Sun than those at higher elevations and near the equator, where sunlight is the most direct. Once sunlight reaches the Earth, it is either reflected back into space or absorbed then released later as *infrared energy* (see Figure 1).

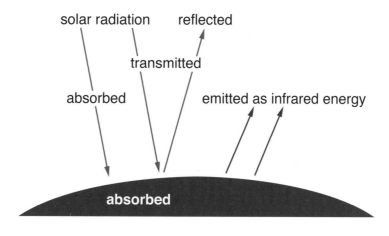

Figure 1

Connections

Sunlight plays a major role in the health of humans. When absorbed by the skin, sunlight enables the body to produce *vitamin D*, a vital nutrient for the body. Vitamin D has been shown to help prevent *osteoporosis*, certain types of cancer, depression, and other mental illnesses. Although vitamin D can be received from dietary supplements, some exposure to natural sunlight is still considered the best way to acquire this essential nutrient.

In addition to vitamin D production, sunlight is very important in developing *circadian rhythms* in many organisms, including humans. Circadian rhythms set the patterns of development, sleep, and daily function on a 24 hour cycle. In humans, the *pineal gland* in the brain, shown in Figure 2, detects sunlight. When sunlight levels are low, the pineal gland releases *melatonin*, a chemical that promotes sleep. This activates a type of "biological clock" that enables people to function on a daily cycle of being awake when it is light and sleeping when it is dark. People who live near the north and south poles and receive limited amounts of sunlight during certain seasons generally have to use artificial Sun lamps in order to regulate their circadian rhythms and promote vitamin D production.

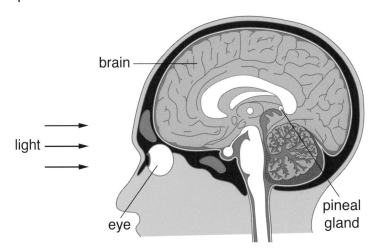

Figure 2

 Want to Know More?

See appendix for Our Findings.

Further Reading

Hutchison, Kristan. "Antarctica's Dome C: Where the Sun's Rays Bounce Back Better." SpaceRef.com, January 8, 2005. Available online. URL:

http://www.spaceref.com/news/viewpr.html?pid=15850. Accessed September 1, 2008. Research in Antarctica helps scientists understand how reflection of sunlight from Earth's surface affects climate.

NASA. "Earth Radiation Budget Facts." Atmospheric Science Data Center, September 28, 2007. Available online. URL: http://eosweb.larc.nasa. gov/EDDOCS/radiation_facts.html. Accessed September 1, 2008. In this concise explanation, NASA points out what happens to the Sun's energy on Earth.

Oklahoma Climatological Survey. "Earth's Energy Budget," 2004. Available online. URL: http://okfirst.mesonet.org/train/meteorology/ EnergyBudget2.html. Accessed September 1, 2008. The amounts of solar radiation absorbed and reflected by Earth are explained.

11. When Fronts Collide

Topic

The behavior of air masses can be demonstrated with water of two different temperatures.

Introduction

Have you ever left home without a jacket on a mild morning, but then regretted it later in the day after a sudden temperature drop? This is because a *cold front* moved through. Cold fronts can move in rapidly and drastically change the weather in an area within a matter of hours. *Warm fronts* tend to move more slowly and bring warmer, more humid air. While warm fronts bring warmer weather, they may also bring steady rain. As a mass of warm air approaches a mass of cooler air, it creates a warm front. Likewise, as a mass of cold air approaches a mass of warmer air, it creates a cold front.

Fronts are the boundaries between two moving masses of air. Whether an air mass is described as *warm* or *cold* depends mostly on its geographic origin. Air masses moving from snowy, polar regions tend to be colder, drier, and faster moving than warm, humid air masses that originated in the tropics. Since there are air masses of varying temperatures throughout the atmosphere, they are constantly in motion trying to come to an equivalence point. In this experiment, you will observe the behavior of colliding fronts using water of different temperatures.

Time Required

20 minutes

Materials

- clear plastic container (approximately 4 inches [in.] by 13 in. [10 centimeters (cm)] by 33 cm)
- 2 pitchers (1 quart each)

- warm tap water
- cold tap water
- red food coloring
- blue food coloring
- spoon
- aluminum foil
- paper towels
- pencil or pen
- science notebook

Safety Note Food coloring can permanently stain clothing. Please review and follow the safety guidelines at the beginning of this volume.

Procedure

1. Fold a piece of aluminum foil so that it fits across the width of the plastic container. Place the foil "barrier" in the center of the container. It should act as a wall separating the container into two sections, but should be able to be removed easily.

2. Fill one pitcher with cold tap water. Add a few drops of blue food coloring and stir with a spoon until it is thoroughly mixed. (*Hint*: avoid adding so much food coloring that the color is deep.)

3. Fill the second pitcher with warm tap water. Add a few drops of red food coloring and stir well until the water is pale red.

4. Pour the red water into one side of the plastic container and the blue water into the other side.

5. Answer Analysis question 1.

6. Remove the foil barrier between the two types of water. Observe what happens and record your observations in your science notebook.

Analysis

1. Write a hypothesis predicting what you think will happen when the warm red water and the cool blue water mix. Justify the reasoning for your hypothesis.

2. What happened when the foil barrier was removed?

3. Why do you think the warm and cool water mixed as they did?

4. Was your hypothesis in question 1 correct? If not, explain why.

5. How is this activity similar to warm and cold air masses mixing in Earth's atmosphere? How is it different?

6. What type of weather can result when fronts collide?

What's Going On?

In warm air, individual air molecules are spread farther apart than those in cold air because warm air molecules have more energy. Therefore, warm air is less dense and moves on top of cooler air when two air masses mix. When fronts collide, one air mass is generally more stationary than the other. The layering of the air at the location of the front depends on which front is approaching and which is receding.

As warm air is forced upward by a wedge of cold air beneath it, the warm air is cooled. As a result, water vapor within the warm air condenses, forming clouds. Clouds are generally formed at any point of any front, but the types of clouds vary depending on what type of front is approaching. When a cold front is approaching, the heavier cold air forms a type of "wedge" under the warm air. The updraft created by this front can form *cumulus clouds*; if it is a strong cold front, it may produce *cumulonimbus clouds*, bringing thunderstorms and drastic drops in temperature. Figure 1 shows what happens when a cold front approaches. When a warm front approaches, the warm air tends to move more gently over the top of the cold air. Layered stratus clouds may develop into *nimbostratus clouds*, which produce rain as shown in Figure 2.

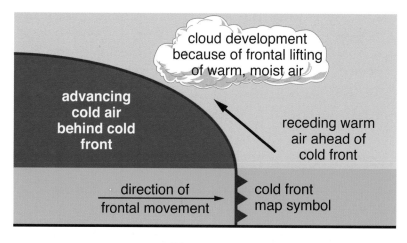

Figure 1

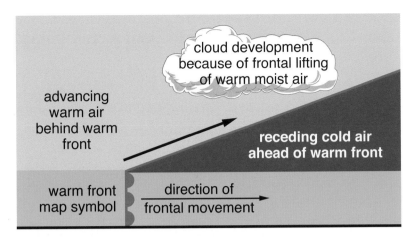

Figure 2

Connections

Sometimes, rapidly approaching cold fronts can produce severe thunderstorms and *tornadoes*. Tornadoes are often formed when cold, dry air moves toward warm, moist air. If the cold front is moving quickly, its collision with the warm front can produce a rotating effect that occurs horizontally near the ground (like the spinning brush of a vacuum cleaner). As the warm air is pushed upward, it cools and condenses into towering cumulonimbus clouds, that are also known as thunderheads. The updraft that produces a thunderhead also pulls the horizontally rotating column of air upward, creating a vertically spinning column of air.

Tornadoes generally form a funnel shape, but can sometimes appear thin and ropelike. They can be very violent and cause massive amounts of damage. Winds from a tornado range from 40 to 160 miles per hour (mph) (64 to 268 kilometers per hour [kph]), but they can exceed 250 mph (420 kph) in severe storms. If a tornado touches down on the ground, it may leave a path of destruction a few miles long. However, some very large tornadoes have caused widespread destruction for nearly 50 miles (80 kilometers [km]).

 ## Want to Know More?

See appendix for Our Findings.

Further Reading

Department of Atmospheric Science, University of Illinois at Urbana-Champaign. "Air Masses and Fronts." Available online. URL: http://

ww2010.atmos.uiuc.edu/(Gh)/guides/mtr/af/home.rxml. Accessed August 30, 2008. This Web site offers excellent pictures and descriptions of different kinds of fronts.

Met Office. "Air Masses." Available online. URL: http://www.metoffice.gov.uk/education/secondary/students/airmasses.html. Accessed August 30, 2008. Met Office provides detailed information on air masses and other topics related to meteorology.

National Oceanic and Atmospheric Administration. "Air Masses." August 29, 2007. Available online. URL: http://www.srh.noaa.gov/jetstream//synoptic/airmass.htm. Accessed on August 30, 2008. Polar air masses and the behavior of warm and cold air masses are explained on this NOAA Web site.

12. How Do Tornadoes Form?

Topic

A tornado chamber can be used to demonstrate the characteristics of a tornado and determine the factors leading to the formation of a tornado.

Introduction

Tornadoes are one of nature's most violent types of storms. Every year in the United States, tornadoes cause widespread destruction and are responsible for hundreds of deaths and billions of dollars of damage. Also known as cyclones or twisters, these storms have a rotating, cyclonic shape. They appear in many shapes, colors, and sizes and can vary in strength, depending on the atmospheric conditions in which they form.

The formation of a tornado is generally associated with a large thunderstorm, known as a *supercell*. This type of thunderstorm has a very strong updraft, which causes an air mass to rotate violently and can give rise to hailstones. A supercell is capable of producing strong tornadoes with winds that can sometimes exceed 300 miles per hour (mph) (483 kilometers per hour [kph]). When tornadoes touch down, they can leave a path of destruction that stretches for miles. Winds from tornadoes can be strong enough to flatten buildings, uproot trees, and carry automobiles for hundreds of yards. The wind speed associated with a tornado is used to classify its intensity on the *Fujita scale*, which ranges from 0 to 5. On the Fujita scale, an F0 tornado has winds that range from 40 to 72 mph (64 to 116 kph), and an F5 tornado has winds that range from 261 to 318 mph (420 to 512 kph). In this experiment, you will create a tornado chamber and observe the characteristics of a tornado.

Time Required

30 minutes

Materials

- 2 clear, empty 2-liter bottles

- washer (1 inch [in.] [2.5 centimeters (cm)] diameter)
- duct tape
- water
- food coloring
- glitter
- pencil or pen
- science notebook

Safety Note Food coloring can permanently stain clothing. Please review and follow the safety guidelines at the beginning of this volume.

Procedure

1. Remove the caps from the two bottles and discard them.
2. Fill one bottle two-thirds full of water. Add a few drops of food coloring and some glitter (this will represent debris and will make your tornado easier to see).
3. Tape the 1-in. (2.5-cm) washer over the top of the bottle that is filled with water. Make sure that the hole in the washer is still open.
4. Take the empty plastic bottle and invert it over the filled one.
5. Tape the two bottles together securely. Wrap the duct tape around the necks of both bottles several times to ensure that no water will leak out (see Figure 1).
6. Turn the chamber upside down so that the filled bottle is on top.
7. Hold the bottles and swirl them several times in a circular motion.
8. Observe your tornado. Repeat as many times as desired. Record your observations in your science notebook.

Analysis

1. Sketch what your tornado looked like.
2. Describe the motion of the tornado you created. What happened when all of the water emptied out of the upper bottle?
3. Why was it necessary to swirl the bottles to create a tornado? What would happen if the bottles were not swirled?

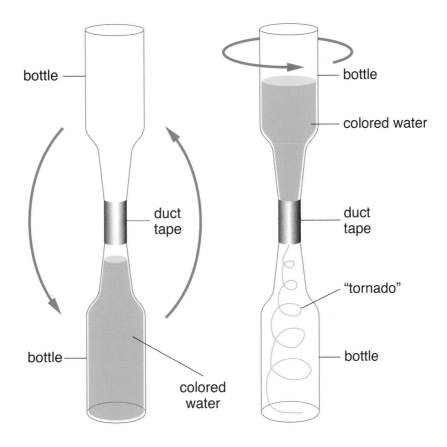

Figure 1

4. What forces were acting on the tornado to make it rotate in the manner that it did?
5. How is your bottle tornado similar to a real tornado in nature? How is it different?
6. Why are the winds associated with a tornado more damaging than wind gusts moving in only one direction?

What's Going On?

Thunderstorms develop when two different fronts combine. If there is a large difference in pressure and temperature, the warmer, lighter air in one front pushes over the cool air of the other front, creating a strong upward draft. Sometimes, the upward draft creates a horizontally rotating region known as a mesocyclone. As rain falls to the ground, it brings cool air with it, creating a downward force called a rear flank downdraft. The strong downdraft can carry the mesocyclone downward as well, resulting in a spiraling cyclone that reaches the ground. At first, a tornado grows in size due to the warm, humid air in the atmosphere that condenses and creates a larger cloud (see Figure 2). This is known as the *mature stage,* and it is the period when a tornado tends to cause the most destruction. Eventually, the twisting nature of the tornado causes the rear flank downdraft to wrap around the tornado, which cuts off the warm air that was "feeding" and powering the storm. At this point, the tornado weakens and eventually dissipates. Occasionally, large supercells are capable of producing multiple tornadoes, either at the same time or in succession.

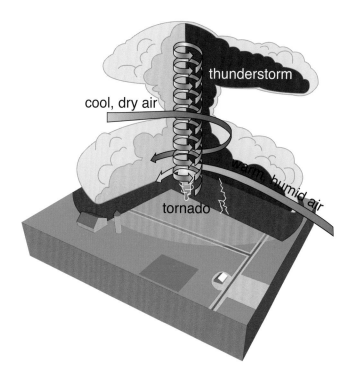

Figure 2

Although all tornadoes share basic characteristics, they can vary in shape, size, and appearance, depending on the atmospheric conditions and the debris picked up by the storm. Some tornadoes can be almost invisible, while others appear dark black. Tornadoes that form over water can form *waterspouts*, which are composed mostly of water. The shape of a mature tornado can range from a narrow funnel a few feet across to a huge wedge with a base that can be more than a mile wide. A tornado's path of destruction can range from several yards to over 100 miles (161 kilometers [km]).

Connections

Tornadoes can be very dangerous, and people are advised to take cover immediately when a tornado is approaching. However, detecting tornadoes is not easy. Prior to the 1950s, tornadoes could only be detected by actually seeing them on the ground. With the onset of weather radar in the early 1960s, *meteorologists* were able to track storm systems and notice any areas of rotation that may produce conditions favorable for tornadoes. When conditions are favorable for tornado development, the weather authorities will issue a *"tornado watch."* Even today there is no way to detect an actual tornado touchdown without visual verification. A *"tornado warning"* can only be issued when a cyclone has actually been spotted.

In the 1970s, the National Weather Service began training individuals to be *storm spotters*. These individuals learn to recognize supercell development and detect the rotation of mesocyclones within a supercell. Storm spotters are generally local police officers, firefighters, state troopers, and other civil servants who observe storms during tornado watches and alert the local weather authority if they see a cyclone. Most cities across the United States have tornado sirens that can be activated during a tornado warning so that individuals can take cover.

Want to Know More?

See appendix for Our Findings.

Further Reading

Cobb, Susan. "Weather Radar." National Oceanic and Atmospheric Administration. Available online. URL: http://www.magazine.noaa.gov/stories/mag151.htm. Accessed August 30, 2008. This Web site presents the history of radar technology in weather forecasting.

Moore, Gene. "Tornadoes, Many Are Different From What Dorothy Saw," Chase Day. Available online. URL: http://www.chaseday.com/tornadoes.htm. Accessed August 30, 2008. Moore provides photographs and explanations of many types of tornadoes.

National Oceanic and Atmospheric Administration. "Tornadoes, Nature's Most Violent Stroms." Available online. URL: http://www.nssl.noaa.gov/edu/safety/tornadoguide.html. Accessed September 12, 2008. The causes and effects of tornadoes are explained very well on this Web site.

13. Temperature and Barometric Pressure

Topic

Measurements of temperature and barometric pressure over a period of time can be used to analyze the relationship of these two weather variables.

Introduction

The Earth's atmosphere is composed of many different air masses that move, collide, and interact to produce the weather systems around the planet. The type and intensity of weather that is created depends on the speed, temperature, pressure, and humidity of the air masses within the atmosphere. The differences in temperature, pressure, humidity, and speed are mostly due to the uneven heating of air by the Sun in different regions of the world, but can be influenced by many other factors as well.

By monitoring the condition and status of different air masses across the planet, meteorologists can predict weather patterns and create a forecast of expected events. One of the most important tools used by meteorologists is a *barometer*. Used to measure atmospheric pressure, a barometer is often a good indicator of upcoming weather. Atmospheric pressure can be linked to many other factors about air masses, including temperature. In this experiment, you will record the temperature and atmospheric pressure in an area for 5 days and determine the extent of the relationship between the two readings.

Time Required

20 minutes on day 1
three 5-minute sessions per day for 5 days (including days 1 and 5)
20 minutes on day 5

Materials

- barometer

- thermometer
- flashlight
- pen or pencil
- graph paper
- ruler
- access to an outdoor area
- science notebook

Safety Note   Please review and follow the safety guidelines at the beginning of this volume.

Procedure

1. Answer analysis questions 1 and 2.

2. Place the barometer and thermometer outside in an easily accessible location.

3. Read the atmospheric pressure from the barometer and the temperature from the thermometer three times on day 1 and record your findings on the data table on page 74. The first readings should be taken in the morning, the second readings should be taken around noon, and the third in the evening (use a flashlight if necessary). (*Note*: Different instruments measure in different units such as Celsius (°C) and Fahrenheit (°F) (temperature) and millimeters or mercury (mmHg) and atmosphere (atm) for pressure. It does not matter which units you choose to use, as long as you are consistent for all readings.)

4. Repeat step 3 for four more days so that you have fifteen readings for pressure and temperature on the data table.

5. Answer Analysis questions 3 through 7.

Analysis

1. State a hypothesis predicting the relationship that you expect to find between temperature and pressure. Justify your reasoning.

2. Drivers often have to add air to their vehicle's tires in the winter to maintain proper air pressure. Why do you think this is? How does this fact relate to your experiment?

Data Table			
Day	Time	Temperature	Pressure
1			
2			
3			
4			
5			

3. Create a scatter graph comparing the temperature and pressure of your readings on graph paper. Be sure to label the graph and all axes.

4. Do you notice a trend on your graph? Explain.

5. What is the relationship of temperature to atmospheric pressure? Does this agree with your hypothesis from question 1?

6. What factors other than temperature could possibly affect atmospheric air pressure? Explain.

7. How can atmospheric pressure be used to predict weather patterns?

What's Going On?

As air is heated, its molecules pick up energy and increase their movement, causing them to spread apart and become less dense. Because hot air is less dense, it rises above cool air. Heating air generally causes pressure to decrease unless the air is in a closed container. In a closed container, rapidly moving air particles collide with the container, increasing the pressure inside the container. However, in the open atmosphere, warm air has lower pressure than cool air.

Air pressure and temperature on the Earth's surface is different from air pressure and temperature higher in the atmosphere. However, both factors have an effect on the conditions that occur on the ground. Other factors, including wind and humidity, also effect air pressure. Winds forcing air up or down within the atmosphere can create areas of high and low pressure that are not directly related to the temperatures on the ground. Storms generally form around areas of low pressure that are created by winds. Humidity can cause air to be more dense and have higher pressure than dry air at the same temperature.

Connections

When warm, low-pressure air meets cool, high-pressure air, it causes wind to blow. This is because warm air, which is less dense than cool air, tends to rise. As the warm air rises, it leaves empty space that can be filled in with cool air. As the cool air rushes to fill the void, it creates wind. Winds generally form between air masses that have a difference in temperature. The *jet stream* is a very large and predominant example of this in North America.

The jet stream is an air current that moves westward in a meandering shape across North America (see Figure 1). It is created by the difference in temperature and pressure between arctic air masses in the north and warm air masses from the south. The jet stream is intensified by the temperature difference between the north and south during the winter, but it tends to be calmer in the summer months. Meteorologists use the jet stream to predict how weather patterns will move across the country. Additionally, commercial airlines use the jet stream to their advantage when flying west because it decreases their flight time dramatically.

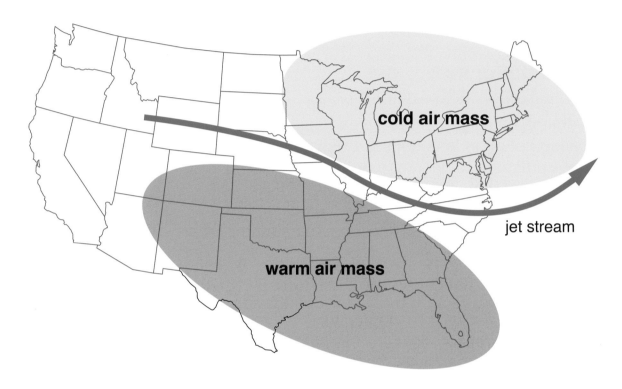

Figure 1

Want to Know More?

See appendix for Our Findings.

Further Reading

Air Spots Net Weather. "Barometric Pressure Map of the United States," November 14, 2001. Available online. URL: http://www.usairnet.com/weather/maps/current/barometric-pressure/. Accessed September 21, 2008. This weather map of the United States shows current barometric readings.

NASA. "It's a Breeze," January 22, 2003. Available online. URL: http://www.kids.earth.nasa.gov/archive/air_pressure/barometer.html. Accessed September 21, 2008. This Web site explains the concept of air pressure.

USA Today. "Understanding Air Pressure," 2008. Available online. URL: http://www.usatoday.com/weather/wbarocx.htm. Accessed September 21, 2008. Written in layman's terms, this article explains air pressure and how it affects weather.

14. How Does Topography Affect Flash Flooding?

Topic

The size and shape of a channel affect the rate at which flooding occurs.

Introduction

According to The Centers for Disease Control and Prevention, flash floods are the number one weather-related cause of death in the United States. A flash flood is the rapid flooding of an area within only a few hours. Generally, flash floods are the result of intense or prolonged periods of rain due to slow-moving thunderstorms, storms repeatedly moving over the same area, or heavy rain due to tropical weather systems such as hurricanes and tropical storms. Rapid flooding may be caused by the oversaturation of the ground after prolonged rainfall, a dam or *levee* breaking, or the release of a large amount of water that built up due to a blockage in a river or stream. Flash flooding usually occurs within 6 hours of a rain event.

Flash floods are often associated with rapidly moving water and can therefore be very dangerous. Flooding can tear down trees, move boulders, carry away cars, destroy buildings, and trap people in their homes. The danger of flash floods is intensified by the fact that they can occur with little or no warning within a very short period of time. Some areas are more prone to flash flooding than others because of their elevation, the soil type, and the topography of the river or stream that could cause the flooding. In this experiment, you will compare the flooding rate of channels of several different shapes and sizes to determine how topography affects the risk of flash flooding.

Time Required

30 minutes

Materials

- poster board

- tape
- aluminum foil
- ruler
- scissors
- modeling clay
- large plastic tub or basin
- gallon jug
- water
- pencil or pen
- science notebook

Safety Note Use caution when working with scissors. Do not splash water near electrical appliances or outlets. Please review and follow the safety guidelines at the beginning of this volume.

Procedure

1. Use ruler, scissors, and poster board to create the sides of three different "channels." Each channel will have a base and two identical side pieces. They should be measured and cut according to the following specifications:

   a. Base: 3 inches (in.) (7.6 centimeters [cm]) by 24in. (61 cm)
      Sides (2): 1 in. (2.5 cm) by 24 in. (61 cm)

   b. Base: 3 in. (7.6 cm) by 24 in. (61 cm)
      Sides (2): 3 in. (7.6 cm) by 24 in. (61 cm)

   c. Base: 3 in. (7.6 cm) by 24 in. (61 cm)
      Sides (2): 5 in. (12.7 cm) by 24 in. (61 cm)

2. Use tape to assemble the channels so that the base rests on the table or counter and the sides stand perpendicular to the base (see Figure 1).

3. Cover the inside of each channel with aluminum foil so that it will be water resistant.

4. Answer Analysis questions 1 through 3.

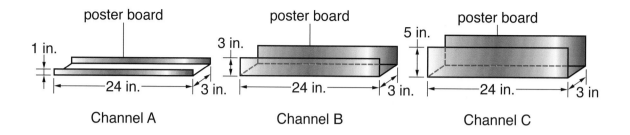

Figure 1

5. Use modeling clay to secure channel A to the bottom of the large plastic container.

6. Take the gallon jug and cut a small hole in the bottom of it for ventilation. Plug the hole with modeling clay, and then fill the jug with water.

7. Have another student stand by with a stopwatch; the student will start time as soon as water begins flowing into the channel and stop it as soon as the water begins to overflow the sides of the channel (not the open ends).

8. Turn the gallon jug completely upside down (not at an angle, as this will affect the flow of water) over the center of the channel and let water pour into the channel.

9. Record the time it took for the channel to overflow on the data table.

10. Repeat steps 5 through 9 with channels B and C, recording all data on the data table.

Data Table	
Channel	**Time (seconds) to overflow**
A	
B	
C	

Analysis

1. List at least five factors that could cause an area to be prone to flash flooding.

2. Do you think that channel shape and size affect the risk of a flash flood? Why or why not?

3. Which of the three channels that you constructed do you think will "flood" the fastest? Why?

4. In the experiment, which channel had the fastest flooding time? Which had the slowest?

5. Describe how the size and shape of the channels you constructed affected the rate at which they overflowed.

6. Suppose there are three rivers that have the same basic shapes as the three channels you created. Assuming that the same amount of rain falls into each channel in the same amount of time, what other factors about the channels would have an effect on the flood rate?

7. Why is it helpful to be able to assess the risk of flash flooding in an area?

What's Going On?

There are several factors that affect the risk of flash flooding in an area. The first and most obvious factor leading to flooding is rainfall. In order to overflow, rivers or streams must receive a large amount of water within a short period of time. Elevation also affects the rate of flash flooding. Since water flows downhill, areas at high elevations are less prone to flooding than flatlands at low elevations. Rivers and streams in low-lying areas are more likely to overflow because they receive runoff from higher elevations nearby. The amount of water that a river or stream can hold depends on the topography of the river, the speed of the water, and the soil type.

Shallow channels tend to flood more easily than deep ones because they cannot contain as much water. If a great deal of water suddenly enters the channel, it has nowhere to go. Likewise, slower-moving rivers tend to flood more quickly than fast-moving ones because water is not removed from the area as quickly. Additionally, the absorbency of the soil in and around a riverbed can affect the rate of flooding. Some types of soil tend to absorb more water than others, and stone and pavement tend to absorb the least water. Therefore, if an area is mostly paved, it cannot absorb as much water from rain, and the rainfall continues to flow into the rivers and they are more likely to flood.

Connections

Intense rainfall can cause flash flooding and other kinds of problems. In order to understand why large amounts of rain fall in a particular area, it is helpful to know a little bit about how rain is formed. Rain is caused by the *condensation* of water vapor into clouds as warm air cools down. However, rainfall patterns often depend on the conditions that caused the rain clouds to form. The manner in which rain is produced classifies it into one of three types: convectional, cyclonic, and orographic (see Figure 2).

Convectional rain generally forms in warm areas during summer. As overheated air rises from the surface of the Earth, it cools rapidly, forming large towering thunderheads. Convectional rain can be intense, but it lasts a very short time. *Cylonic rain* is caused by the collision of fronts, or masses of air. When warm air meets cooler air, the warm air rises above the dense, cool air and form clouds. Often, because of the collision of fronts, the clouds will form in a rotating manner, forming a cyclonic shape and producing intense rainfall that lingers over an area for several hours to several days. Finally, *orographic rain* is formed due to the geography of an area. When air passes over mountains, it is forced upward and it begins to condense into clouds. These clouds can cause steady rain seasonally or throughout the year in particular areas, but causes areas on the other side of the mountain range to remain dry. Flash flooding is most often caused by cyclonic rain, but can also result from convection rain. Due to the continual nature of orographic rain, areas that receive this type of rainfall have adjusted to the amount of water they receive and flooding rarely occurs.

Want to Know More?

See appendix for Our Findings.

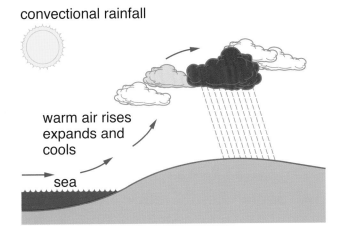

convectional rainfall

warm air rises
expands and
cools

sea

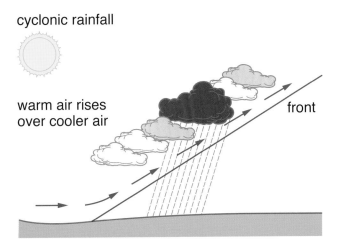

cyclonic rainfall

warm air rises
over cooler air

front

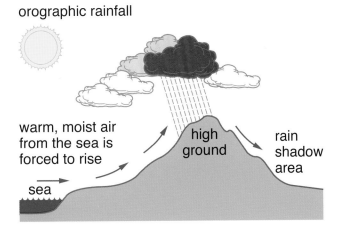

orographic rainfall

warm, moist air
from the sea is
forced to rise

high
ground

rain
shadow
area

sea

Figure 2

Further Reading

Doesken, Nolan J., and Thomas B. McKee. "An Analysis of Rainfall for the July 28, 1997, Flood in Fort Collins, Colorado," Colorado Climate Center. Available online. URL: http://ccc.atmos.colostate.edu/~odie/rain.html. Accessed September 21, 2008. Written for upper-level students, this report explains how the topography of the Fort Collins, Colorado, area contributed to flooding.

National Oceanic and Atmospheric Administration. "Basic Heavy Rain/ Flash Flood Concepts," September 21, 2004. Available online. URL: http://www.crh.noaa.gov/lmk/soo/docu/rain.php. Accessed September 21, 2008. This Web site explains how factor such as amount of precipitaion and topography affect flash flooding.

ScienceDaily. "Scientists Test System to Forecast Flash Floods Along Colorado's Front Range," July 28, 2008. Available online. URL: http://www.sciencedaily.com/releases/2008/07/080722143710.htm. Accessed September 21, 2008. A new forecasting system helps meteorologists pinpoint regions that are vulnerable to flash floods.

15. How Accurate Are Weather Predictions?

Topic

The accuracy with which meteorologists can predict the weather varies.

Introduction

How do you know whether or not to carry your umbrella or wear a heavy jacket before you even step outside? More than likely, you check the weather forecast. The scientists who study the conditions and patterns within the atmosphere in order to develop weather forecasts are called *meteorologists*.

Humans have attempted to predict weather since the beginning of civilization, mostly relying on cloud and wind patterns and astrology. Meteorologists today use scientific tools to develop long-term and short-term forecasts. These tools include weather balloons to measure existing conditions and weather modeling computer programs that analyze weather conditions and predict future events. Although weather forecasting has come a long way due to modern technological advances, it is still not an exact science. In this experiment, you will obtain predictions from different meteorologists, measure the actual weather conditions, and compare the accuracy of the meteorologists' predictions.

Time Required

30 minutes on day 1
two 10-minute periods per day for 5 additional days

Materials

- outdoor thermometer
- rain gauge
- local 5-day weather forecasts from 3 sources
- pen or pencil
- science notebook

> **Safety Note**   Please review and follow the safety guidelines at the beginning of this volume.

Procedure

1. Obtain three 5-day detailed weather forecasts for the days on which you will perform your observations. Detailed forecasts (giving predictions for certain times of day) are usually only available 1 to 2 days in advance, so you may have to access the forecast on TV or the Internet several times within the 5-day period. Be sure to have the predictions before taking your measurements.

2. Set up the thermometer and rain gauge in an outdoor location where they will not be disturbed.

3. Choose two specific times that you will take temperature and precipitation readings daily.

4. Record the forecasted conditions for these specific times on Data Table 1. Be sure to include temperature, precipitation chance, cloud cover, and comments.

5. At the times chosen, go outside and check the weather:

    a. Take a reading from the thermometer. Record the temperature on Data Table 2.

    b. Check the rain gauge to see if any precipitation has fallen. Record precipitation on Data Table 2. Empty the rain gauge after each reading.

    c. Observe cloud cover and sky conditions. Make note of any dark clouds, fog, strong winds, and any other conditions. Record the information on Data Table 2.

    d. Record any additional observations that are relevant.

6. Repeat step 4 twice a day for 5 consecutive days.

Analysis

1. For each of the forecasted temperatures, find the absolute value difference in the predicted temperature and the actual temperature from your readings. For instance, if the prediction was 64 degrees fahrenheit (°F) (18 degrees Celsius [°C]) and the actual temperature was 62°F (17°C), the difference would be 2. Record the absolute difference for each reading on Data Table 3.

Data Table 1

Forecast 1   **Meteorologist** _____

	Day 1		Day 2		Day 3		Day 4		Day 5	
Time										
Temperature										
Precipitation										
Sky conditions										
Other notes										

Forecast 2   **Meteorologist** _____

	Day 1		Day 2		Day 3		Day 4		Day 5	
Time										
Temperature										
Precipitation										
Sky conditions										
Other notes										

Forecast 3   **Meteorologist** _____

	Day 1		Day 2		Day 3		Day 4		Day 5	
Time										
Temperature										
Precipitation										
Sky conditions										
Other notes										

Data Table 2										
	Day 1		Day 2		Day 3		Day 4		Day 5	
Time										
Temperature										
Precipitation										
Sky conditions										
Other notes										

2. Find the average difference in temperature by adding the numbers in each row of Data Table 3 and dividing by 10. Record the average difference in the last column of Data Table 3.

3. Which meteorologist had the most accurate temperature predictions?

Data Table 3										
	Day 1		Day 2		Day 3		Day 4		Day 5	
Time										Avg
Meteorologist 1; Difference										
Meteorologist 2; Difference										
Meteorologist 3; Difference										

4. Observe the predictions for other conditions, such as rain, cloud cover, and other factors noted in your comments. Which meteorologist had the most accurate predictions for these conditions?

5. Why do you think some meteorologists might have different weather forecasts for the same area?

6. How do meteorologists come up with forecasts? What tools do they use?

7. Is it possible to perfectly predict future weather conditions? Why or why not?

What's Going On?

When formal weather forecasting began in the 19th century, predictions were based mostly upon barometric pressure, sky conditions, and current weather conditions. These factors are still important today, but modern meteorologists input data into a computerized forecast model, which uses mathematical equations to predict future weather occurrences. Forecast models use data from weather balloons, satellite imagery, and readings of surface conditions such as temperature, humidity, and pressure to begin their calculations of forecasted conditions. The mathematical equations not only factor in current weather data, but they also account for the probability of certain events occurring based on historical weather patterns.

Even though meteorologists have developed complex technological devices to measure atmospheric conditions from Earth as well as from space, and are able to use computerized forecasting models, predictions are still not always accurate. Modern forecast models account for the chaotic nature of weather to some extent, but they cannot tell exactly what will occur when air masses collide in the atmosphere; they can only predict what is most likely to happen. Some meteorologists may predict weather more accurately than others because of very precise data collection tools and accurate input, but a portion of forecasting is simply up to chance.

Connections

When you hear on the news about the threat of an approaching storm, you will most likely see a weather radar image such as the one in Figure 1. *Doppler radar* creates most of the images you see on television showing the approach of storms. The Doppler effect, named after Austrian physicist Christian Doppler (1803–53), is the change in frequency and wavelength of a sound wave depending on the location of the source and the observer. Doppler radar uses sound waves produced by an antenna, which "bounce" off of objects such as dust particles or rain drops and then return to the antenna. Using the frequency and wavelength of the sound waves that return, Doppler radar can develop images showing the concentration of clouds and precipitation as well as their location.

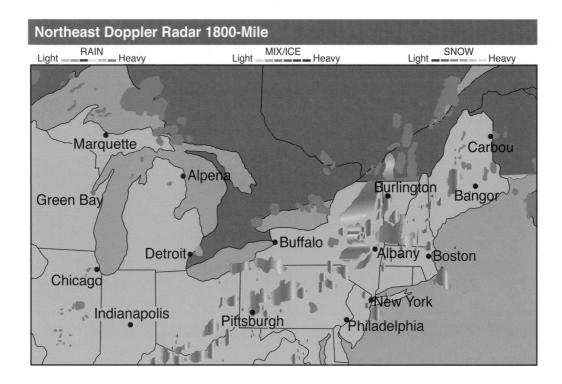

Figure 1

The National Weather Service installed Doppler radar systems across the United States in the 1980s and early 1990s. Today, many television stations have their own Doppler radar systems. Meteorologists use Doppler radar to track local weather systems as well as those developing in other parts of the country which may produce inclement weather in the future. This type of system is very helpful in understanding the weather that is currently happening and can help meteorologists in predicting the weather that will occur within the next few hours or days.

 Want to Know More?

See appendix for Our Findings.

Further Reading

NASA. "New NASA Data Helps Take 'Whether' Out of Weather Prediction," April 29, 2003. Available online. URL: http://www.jpl.nasa.gov/news/news.cfm?release=2003-063. Accesed August 30, 2008. This Web site shows how weather instruments aboard NASA's satellites improve the accuracy of weather forecasts.

National Oceanic and Atmospheric Administration. "The History of Numerical Weather Condition," June 4, 2007. Available online. URL: http://celebrating200years.noaa.gov/foundations/numerical_wx_pred/welcome.html. Accessed August 30, 2008. This NOAA Web page explains how numerical weather predictions use mathematical models to help forecast weather.

Science Daily. "Perfect Weather Conditions," May 1, 2008. Available online. URL: http://www.sciencedaily.com/videos/2008/0507-perfect_weather_predictions.htm. Accessed August 30, 2008. Improvements in weather forecasting are discussed on this Web page.

16. How Much Dew Forms at Night?

Topic

The amount of dew that forms on a square meter of the ground can be correlated to humidity and air temperature.

Introduction

Have you ever left something outside overnight only to find it wet the next morning? The water you find on objects in the morning is most likely dew formed by the condensation of water vapor from the air. Formation of dew is similar to the *condensation* of water on the outside of a beaker containing ice water (see Figure 1).

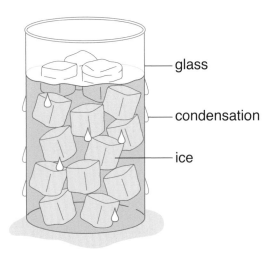

glass

condensation

ice

Figure 1

During the day, the heating of the Earth by the Sun causes water to evaporate. After the Sun goes down, surfaces on Earth begin to cool. These cooler surfaces cause water vapor to change from a gas into a liquid. The amount of dew that forms depends on the amount of *humidity*, or water vapor in the air, as well as the change in temperature overnight. In this laboratory, you will design an experiment to determine the relationship between dew and humidity by observing the formation of dew over several days.

Time Required

30 minutes per day for 5 days (time required will vary depending on student experiment)

Materials

- wool fabric (about 3 yards [yd] by 3 yd or 1 meter [m] by 1 m)
- 4 nails (at least 3 inches [in.] [7.62 centimeters (cm)] long)
- meterstick
- triple-beam balance or electronic scale
- thermometer
- hygrometer
- graduated cylinder
- graph paper
- access to an outdoor area
- science notebook

Safety Note   Use caution when working with nails and when using electronic appliances near water. Please review and follow the safety guidelines at the beginning of this volume.

Procedure

1. Your job is to design and perform an experiment to find out how the humidity during the day and the change in temperature overnight are related to the amount of dew that forms.

2. You can use any of the materials provided by your teacher, but you will not need to use all of them.

3. Before you conduct your experiment, decide exactly what you are going to do. Write the steps you plan to take (your experimental procedure) and the materials you plan to use (materials list) on the Data Table 1. Show your procedure and materials list to your teacher. If you get teacher approval, proceed with your experiment. If not, modify your work and show it to your teacher again.

Data Table 2	
Dew point	**Perception**
52 & lower	comfortable
53-56	slightly noticeable
57-59	quite noticeable
60-63	sticky
64-69	uncomfortable
70 +	extremely uncomfortable

Connections

Sometimes, plants may have water droplets on their leaves in the morning when the dew point was not reached overnight. In fact, the water drops on plants are not always caused by dew. Sometimes, plants release water from their leaves through *guttation,* which occurs when the root pressure of plants forces water upward through a plant. At night, when evaporation is low, the water is simply pushed through the pores in the leaves, where it remains until morning.

Guttation in plants is related to *transpiration*, the process of water movement through a plant. Water enters plants through their roots, and it exits through the leaves by evaporation. When water evaporates from leaves, it creates the same type of suction as a straw does, drawing more water up the stalk of the plant. This process is aided by *root pressure*, caused by the buildup of water in the roots, which forces water upward. Transpiration decreases when the Sun goes down because less evaporation occurs. However, guttation does not necessarily cease when transpiration does. If the root pressure is high, excess water is forced out of a plant through the leaves, causing water droplets that appear very similar to dew.

 **Want to Know More?**

See appendix for Our Findings.

Further Reading

Friedlander, Blaine P. "Why Northeast's Hot Spell Was So Draining: Dew Point Exceeded Air-Conditioning Designs, According to Cornell Climate Experts," Cornell University News Services, July 26, 2005. Available online. URL: http://www.news.cornell.edu/stories/July05/NRCC-dewpoints.bpf.html. Accessed September 1, 2008. Friedlander explains how the dew point affects the way we feel.

Weather Savvy. "What Exactly Is the Dew Point?" Available online. URL: http://weathersavvy.com/Q-dew_point1.html. Accessed September 1, 2008. This Web site provides a clear explanation of dew point and its relationship to temperature and humidity.

Weather Underground. "U.S. Dew Point," 2008. Available online. URL: http://www.wunderground.com/US/Region/US/Dewpoint.html. Accessed September 1, 2008. Students can check the current dew points nationwide on this Web site.

17. Does Sunset Color Vary With Weather Conditions?

Topic

The color of the sunset can be correlated to local weather conditions.

Introduction

Sunset is one of the most spectacular times of the day. At times, a sunset will be so vividly colored that it appeared to have been painted in the sky. The hues of sunsets can vary from yellows and oranges, to pinks, purples, and reds (see Figure 1). The different colors that we see are due to the way that light is scattered as the Sun moves farther away.

Figure 1
Sunset

As the Sun sets, it appears to drop low in the sky, and then it disappears from our sight. Actually, the Sun is not moving downward. In fact, it is not the movement of the Sun that creates sunsets; they are due to Earth's rotation. The Earth continually rotates counterclockwise so that some areas are facing the Sun, while others are facing away from it. When the Earth rotates so that the Sun is no longer shining on an area, the Sun appears to "set" in the western sky. As the Sun disappears below the horizon, it takes on reddish orange colors that reflect off of the clouds. The colors that appear when light is reflected in a sunset depend on the location of the sunset as well as the weather and atmospheric conditions in the area. In this experiment, you will observe the sunset and weather conditions for several days and determine how the weather affects sunset colors.

Time Required

30 minutes per day for 5 days

Materials

- thermometer
- barometer
- hygrometer
- digital or instant camera
- access to an outdoor space for observing the sunset
- access to a meteorology text that includes pictures of cloud types
- science notebook

Safety Note   Please review and follow the safety guidelines at the beginning of this volume.

Procedure

1. Choose a location from which to watch the sunset for 5 days. (If possible, select a location where the Sun will set over the water, because the reflection intensifies the colors.)

2. Answer Analysis question 1.

3. Set up the thermometer, barometer, and hygrometer in the location where you will be doing your observations. If you are viewing the sunset from a park or other public place, you may have to remove your weather instruments and set them up again every time you come to observe the sunset.

4. Record the temperature, atmospheric pressure, relative humidity, types of clouds in the sky, amount of cloud cover, and any other observations of the current weather conditions on the data table.

5. Watch the sunset. As the Sun appears to approach the horizon, record the colors that you see on the data table. Take a picture to use for analysis and comparison later. Continue observing until the sky turns mostly dark.

6. Repeat steps 2 through 4 for four more days, take pictures, and record your observations on the data table.

7. Finish answering the Analysis questions.

Analysis

1. Write a hypothesis predicting how the weather conditions will affect the colors of the sunset at dusk.

2. During each sunset, when did the most dramatic colors appear?

3. Observe the pictures you took of the sunset each day and describe how the colors changed from day to day.

4. Is there a relationship between the weather observations you made and the colors of the sunset? Explain.

5. Do your results agree with your hypothesis from Analysis question 1? Explain why or why not.

6. What other conditions may affect sunset color in addition to the weather?

What's Going On?

Visible light from the Sun is described as white light. When white light passes through molecules, water droplets, or a prism, it is *diffracted*, or separated, into different colors. During the day, when the Sun is overhead, light only passes through a few miles of atmosphere. Gas molecules in the atmosphere absorb some of the light from the Sun. Most of the longer wavelengths pass through the molecules, but the shorter wavelengths such as blue, are reflected. Therefore, the sky appears to be blue on a clear day because the blue light is reflected.

At sunset, light travels a much longer distance through the atmosphere. Blue light is reflected multiple times so that it scatters instead of being reflected directly back to a person watching the sunset. Therefore, the dominant colors in a sunset are those at the end of the *visible light*

Data Table

Day	Temperature	Atmospheric pressure	Humidity	Type of clouds	Amount of cloud cover	Other weather observations	Colors present in sunset	Description of sunset
1								
2								
3								
4								
5								

> **Safety Note**   Use caution when operating the hot plate so that you do not burn yourself. Be careful using water near electrical outlets and appliances. Rubbing alcohol is flammable and should not be used near a hot plate. Please review and follow the safety guidelines at the beginning of this volume.

Procedure

1. Add equal parts of rubbing alcohol and tap water to a clear plastic bottle. Add a few drops of food coloring to the liquid in the bottle and mix well.

2. Using a ruler, draw markings along a clear plastic straw beginning about one-fourth of the way from one end. The markings should be a uniform distance apart; this will serve as your custom temperature scale where each mark represents 1 degree.

3. Place the straw into the bottle so that the first mark you created lines up with the top of the liquid. Make sure that the straw is not touching the bottom of the bottle.

4. Secure the straw in place with modeling clay.

5. Record the "temperature" from your homemade thermometer in the "Room temperature" column on the data table.

6. Measure the temperature in Celsius and Fahrenheit and record these on the data table as well.

7. Set up an ice bath by placing ice and water into a beaker. Set up a hot water bath using the hot plate to warm some water in the other beaker.

8. Place your thermometer as well as a Celsius and Fahrenheit thermometer into the ice bath.

9. After 10 minutes, record the temperatures from all three thermometers on the data table.

10. Place all three thermometers into the hot water bath for 10 minutes and record the temperatures on the data table.

Analysis

1. What happened to the liquid in the straw when the temperature rose?

Data Table			
Thermometer	**Temperature in ice water**	**Room temperature**	**Hot water temperature**
Your temperature scale			
Celsius			
Fahrenheit			

2. Why do you think the liquid moved the way that it did when the temperature changed?

3. Why was tap water (rather than pure water) used in the thermometer?

4. How did your temperature scale compare to the temperature in Celsius? In Fahrenheit?

5. To convert from Celsius to Fahrenheit, the formula is $F = (9/5)\ C + 32$. Do your temperature readings agree with this formula?

6. Using the difference between thermometer readings on your scale and the Celsius thermometer readings, create a conversion factor that will convert your temperature readings into Celsius.

7. Create a conversion factor between your temperature scale and Fahrenheit.

What's Going On?

The German physicist Gabriel Fahrenheit (1686–1736) created the first thermometers in the early 1700s. Originally, he used a glass tube with a bulb at the end filled with alcohol. Alcohol expands faster than water when it is heated, and rises in the tube at a predictable rate. Later, after studying the expanding properties of mercury, Fahrenheit created the mercury thermometer that used a narrow cylinder instead of a round bulb. The Fahrenheit temperature scale was named in his honor. In the mid-

1700s, the Swedish astronomer Anders Celsius (1701–44) created the Centigrade or Celsius scale. He calibrated thermometers so that they read 0° at the freezing point of water and 100° at water's boiling point.

Fahrenheit and Celsius were not the only two men interested in measuring temperature. At one time, several different temperature scales were in use. The list of scales included the Reaumur, Romer, Newton, Leyden, Wedgewood, Hales, Ducrest, and Edinburgh. During the 18th century, one thermometer might have four different temperature scales inscribed on it. Today, all but the basic three have fallen out of favor.

Since the 1700s, many types of thermometers have been created. While many medical and scientific thermometers use glass tubes filled with mercury or alcohol, other types of thermometers use a multitude of different substances such as gas, liquid crystals, or electrical resistance. To make reading thermometers convenient, many modern devices have digital output that gives instantaneous temperature readings. These readings are shown by an electronic chip that was calibrated to read and output temperatures according to a given scale.

Connections

The Earth's atmosphere prevents drastic temperature differences between day and night. However, temperatures around the planet can vary drastically with location. Antarctica remains frozen year-round, while cities along the equator never reach freezing temperatures. The temperature of an area depends on several factors, including its latitude, altitude, distance from the sea, and the prevailing winds in the area.

The Earth is warmed by energy from the Sun. Because the equator receives more sunlight than other regions, temperatures are much warmer at the equator than at the poles. Therefore, areas that are close to the equator are much warmer year-round than places that are farther away. Additionally, due to the tilt of the Earth, the temperate regions between the equator and poles experience seasons. The Northern Hemisphere experiences summer when it is tilted closer to the Sun than the Southern Hemisphere. Winter occures in the Northern Hemisphere when it is tilted farther away from the Sun (see Figure 2). The opposite occurs in the Southern Hemisphere.

An area's temperature also depends on its altitude. Mountainous regions tend to be cooler than places that are lower in elevation. This is because the Sun warms the Earth's surface, which in turn warms the atmosphere.

High elevations, which are farther from the surface, experience cooler temperatures. In addition, places that are closer to the ocean are cooler than those in the center of a continent—the Sun warms landmasses much faster than bodies of water, so inland regions are warmer than coastal ones. Temperatures are also influenced by prevailing winds, which are moving air masses created by temperature and pressure differences. The temperature of prevailing winds depends on the area in which they originated. Arctic prevailing winds can bring very cold weather patterns south of the Arctic, while prevailing winds originating near the equator bring warm weather to otherwise temperate regions.

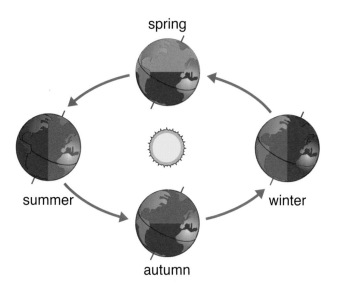

Figure 2

Want to Know More?

See appendix for Our Findings.

Further Reading

Brain, Marshall. "How Thermometers Work," HowStuffWorks, 2008. Available online. URL: http://www.howstuffworks.com/therm. htm. Accessed September 1, 2008. Brain explains thermometer technology.

Day, Martha Marie, and Anthony Carpi. "Temperature," Vision Learning, 2008. Available online. URL: http://www.visionlearning.com/library/module_viewer.php?mid=48. Accessed September 1, 2008. A good discussion on the three types of thermometers and pictures of each type are found on this Web site.

Radford, Tim. "A Brief History of Thermometers," *Guardian*. August 6, 2003. Available online. URL: http://www.guardian.co.uk/science/2003/ aug/06/weather.environment. Accessed September 1, 2008. Radford explains how Fahrenheit, Celsius, and Kelvin developed their temperature scales.

19. A Convection Box

Topic

A convection box demonstrates convection currents and temperature inversions.

Introduction

When you open the refrigerator door, you probably feel cold air pouring out. This refrigerated air sinks toward your feet instead of rising toward the ceiling because cold air is denser than warm air. *Density* is the amount of matter present per unit volume. The cold air from the refrigerator behaves just like cold air in the atmosphere.

Sunlight striking the Earth warms the air near its surface. Warming transfers energy to the air, causing air molecules to pick up speed. As they move, the molecules spread out and the air becomes less dense than surrounding air. Because of the decrease in its density, the warmed air becomes *buoyant*, or able to float or rise through the surrounding air. As a result, warmed air rises during the day. At night, the air cools and sinks back toward the Earth (see Figure 1). This cyclic behavior of air rising and sinking creates *convection currents*, air flows that are due to differences in density. In some cases, this typical movement of air is obstructed by a *temperature inversion,* a situation that occurs when warm air moves over cool air, trapping it. In this experiment, you will find out how convection currents and temperature inversions form.

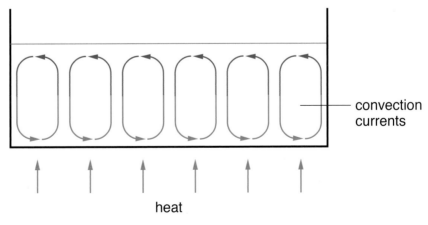

convection currents

heat

Figure 1

Time Required

55 minutes

Materials

- large shoe box
- 2 cardboard tubes (such as paper towel tubes)
- aluminum foil
- tape
- glue
- scissors
- plastic wrap
- small candle (such as a tea light candle)
- long match
- 2 paper towels
- 2 small plastic bags
- 4 to 6 ice cubes
- gooseneck lamp with bulb (60 watts or more)
- index card
- science notebook

Safety Note   Use caution when using matches and candles. Please review and follow the safety guidelines at the beginning of this volume.

Procedure

1. Working with a partner, remove the lid from the shoe box and set the lid aside.

2. Stand the shoe box on its side. Cut two holes in the side of the box facing up, one at each end. Each hole should be just large enough to hold a cardboard tube.

3. Push a cardboard tube into each hole. Seal the area around each tube with tape so that it is airtight. Each tube will serve as a chimney.

4. Line the shoe box and the chimneys with aluminum foil. Either tape or glue the aluminum foil in place.

5. Simulate the formation of convection currents. To do so:

    a. Position a small candle in the box directly under one of the chimneys. Make sure that the candle is at least 3 inches (in.) (7.6 centimeters [cm]) below the tube.

    b. Tape clear plastic wrap over the open side of the shoe box so that you can view the inside of the box. Be sure to form an airtight seal as you tape the plastic wrap in place.

    c. Light the long match; then carefully lower it through the chimney over the candle and light the candle. Take care not to touch the shoe box or cardboard chimney with the burning match. Remove and blow out the match.

    d. Let the candle burn for about five minutes to warm the interior of the shoe box.

    e. Tightly wad a paper towel, then light it. After the paper towel burns a few seconds, extinguish it.

    f. Hold the smoking paper towel over the chimney without the candle. Observe the behavior of the smoke and record your observations in your science notebook.

6. Simulate a temperature inversion. To do so:

    a. Put two or three ice cubes in each small plastic bag. Do not overfill the bags; they must be able to fit into the chimneys.

    b. Extinguish the candle.

    c. Lower a plastic bag of ice cubes through each chimney. Drop the bags of ice cubes into the shoe box.

    d. Let the interior of the box cool for a few minutes

    e. After the box has cooled, turn on the lamp and position it over one chimney. Leave it in place for about 5 minutes.

    f. Tightly wad a paper towel, then light it. After the paper towel burns a few seconds, extinguish it.

    g. Drop the smoking paper towel down the other chimney (the one without the lamp). Immediately cover this chimney with an index card. Observe the behavior of the smoke and record your observations in your science notebook.

h. Lift the index card from the unheated chimney. Observe the smoke and record your observations.

Analysis

1. What is a convection current?
2. What is a temperature inversion?
3. Why do you think that smoking paper towels were used in this experiment?
4. What happened to the smoke in step 5?
5. What happened to the smoke in step 6?

What's Going On?

Convection is the transfer of heat by currents in liquids or gases. The Sun's rays warm air on the Earth's surface. This warm air rises, creating a convection current. In step 5 of this experiment, smoke was pulled into the box through one chimney. Inside the box, the smoky air warmed, then rose and exited through the second chimney. This demonstration shows what happens to air in regions near the equator, which receive more of the Sun's energy than areas near the poles. Warm, less-dense air from the equatorial zones rises and moves toward the poles, where air is denser and heavier. This movement causes constant convection currents known as *convection cells* (see Figure 2).

A temperature inversion occurs when warm air moves over cool air, trapping it. In the experiment, ice cubes were used to cool the air in the box. A lamp provided the heat to create a layer of warm air on top of the cooled air. As a result, a normal convection current could not be established.

Connections

As a general rule, air temperature decreases as altitude increases. As a result, air moves up in the atmosphere, carrying with it any pollutants or particles. This typical movement of air helps disperse air pollutants and keep air near the Earth's surface relatively clear.

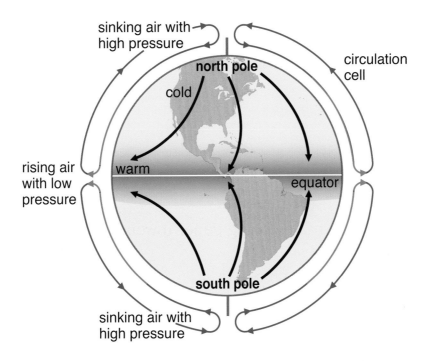

Figure 2

Temperature inversions are abnormal situations that can create real problems by trapping air pollution close to the surface. A temperature inversion forms when very cool air moves in under warm, rising air. Sources of exceptionally cool air include winds from cool regions of the ocean or cold air moving down the slope of a mountain (see Figure 3). In either case, the warm air forms a blanket over the cooler air, trapping it near the surface. Since the cooler air is denser than the warm air, the two layers do not mix. Such a situation can hold air close to the Earth for days. If the trapped air is in a city, air pollutants from cars, businesses, and homes can build up quickly. These pollutants can create *smog*, a mixture of emissions and particles that can lead to itchy eyes and respiratory problems.

Want to Know More?

See appendix for Our Findings.

Further Reading

Environmental Protection Authority Victoria. "What is Smog?" July 17, 2006. Available online. URL: http://www.epa.vic.gov.au/air/aq4kids/

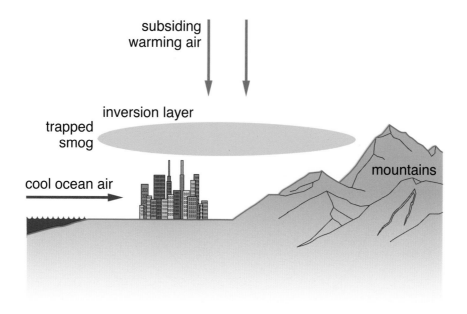

Figure 3

smog.asp. Accessed September 21, 2008. This Web site explains how summer and winter smog form and how they can be trapped by temperature inversions.

National Oceanic and Atmospheric Administration. "What Are Temperature Inversions?" Available online. URL: http://www.wrh.noaa.gov/slc/climate/TemperatureInversions.php. Accessed September 21, 2008. The National Weather Service, through NOAA, provides information on all weather topics.

Stern, David P. "Weather and the Atmosphere," From Stargazers to Starships, September 22, 2004. Available online. URL: http://iki.rssi.ru/mirrors/stern/stargaze.Sintro.htm. Accessed September 21 2008. Dr. Stern's "book-on-the-web" provides information on meteorology and other topics.

20. Intensity of Insolation

Topic

The degree of insolation affects the amount of solar energy an area receives.

Introduction

What region would you guess has the coolest average yearly temperature: Quito, Ecuador, near the equator, Dallas, Texas, in the southwestern United States, or Nome, Alaska, west of Canada? You probably know the answer to that question. Nome, Alaska, is much colder than the other two locations. One of the factors that affects Nome's temperature is the angle at which the Sun's rays strike the Earth, a property know as angle of solar radiation or intensity of *insolation*.

When the Sun is directly overhead, solar energy strikes the Earth at a 90-degree angle. The only places where the Sun can truly be overhead are located near the equator, between the tropic of Cancer and the tropic of Capricorn (see Figure 1). However, all points on Earth experience periods when the Sun is at a higher angle in the sky than at other times. The position of the Sun and the angle at which the Sun's rays strike Earth have an impact on surface temperatures, weather, and climate. In this experiment, you will find out how the angle of insolation affects the intensity of light energy striking the planet.

Time Required

55 minutes

Materials

- flashlight
- graph paper
- ruler

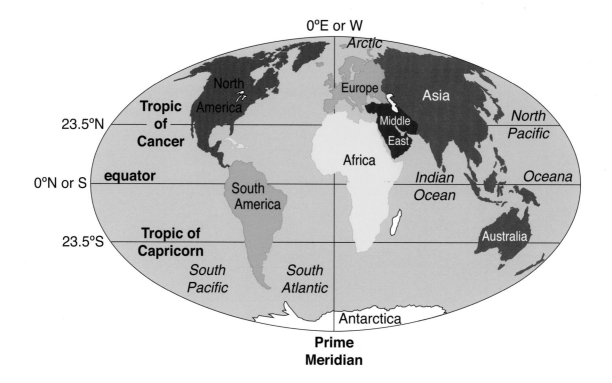

Figure 1

- ◆ protractor
- ◆ thermometer
- ◆ stopwatch
- ◆ science notebook

Procedure

1. Divide a piece of graph paper into three sections. Label the sections A, B, and C.
2. Place the graph paper on the desktop. Stand the protractor on section A of the graph paper.
3. Working with a partner, position the ruler so that it is standing straight up on the paper, at the 90-degree line on the protractor (see Figure 2).

4. Turn on the flashlight and hold it at a 90-degree angle on the protractor so that it shines straight down on the paper.

5. Use a pencil to outline the beam of light striking the paper. (If the light beam has an intense region and a less intense region, outline the intense region only.)

6. Place the thermometer bulb in the center of the beam of light striking the paper. Leave the thermometer in place for 3 minutes. Read the temperature and record the temperature in the appropriate row on the data table.

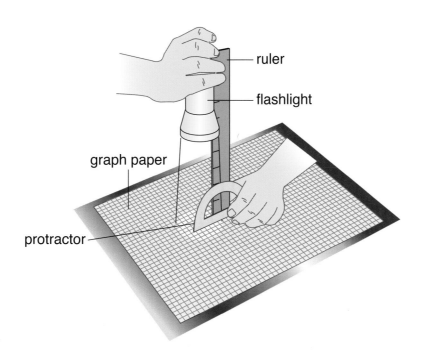

Figure 2

7. Set aside the flashlight, ruler, and protractor. Count the number of squares within the outline. Record this number on the data table.

8. Repeat steps 2 through 7 on section B of the graph paper, but position the ruler and flashlight at the 66-degree angle on the protractor.

9. Repeat steps 2 through 7 on section C of the graph paper, but position the ruler and flashlight at the 33-degree angle on the protractor.

Data Table		
Position of flashlight	**Temperature**	**Number of squares covered**
90° angle		
66° angle		
33° angle		

Analysis

1. At which angle, 90-degree, 66-degree, or 33-degree, was the beam of light smallest and most intense on the graph paper?

2. At what angle was the beam of light largest and most diffuse on the graph paper?

3. At what angle was the temperature the highest?

4. At what angle was the temperature the lowest?

5. Based on your finding, what is the correlation between angle of insolation and temperature?

What's Going On?

Life on Earth relies on energy from the Sun. Not every region of Earth receives the same amount of solar energy. Therefore, different regions have different climates, each of which supports unique types of organisms. Temperature is an important characteristic of climate.

One factor that affects temperature on our planet is angle of insolation. When the Sun is vertical, or straight overheat, the angle of insolation is 90 degrees. At this time, the Earth receives the maximum amount of energy. As the angle of insolation decreases, the Sun's rays are spread over a larger area and the intensity of solar energy in that area decreases. At lower angles, sunlight has to travel a longer distance through the atmosphere to reach Earth. Consequently, the light energy has more opportunities to encounter particles that deflect or absorb the energy.

Connections

Three factors influence the angle of insolation for any area: time of day, season, and *latitude*. Angle of insolation increases from morning to noon, so the Sun's rays are closest to vertical at noon. This is the time of day that Earth receives the most intense sunlight. From noon to evening, the angle of insolation increases. Despite this, noon may not be the hottest time of day. From noon to late afternoon, the lower atmosphere absorbs a lot of the Sun's heat. Therefore, the temperature continues to rise. After dark, the Earth's surface begins to cool, radiating heat. The coolest hour is usually just before dawn.

Seasons affect angle of insolation because the position of the Earth's axis relative to the Sun changes. This variation influences the intensity of light rays striking Earth's surface. At 45 degrees, the area receiving radiation is about 40 percent larger than at 90 degrees. This increase in area reduces the intensity of light by approximately 30 percent. During summer, the angle of insolation for any area is at its maximum.
As latitude increases, the angle of insolation decreases. Notice in Figure 3 that latitude at the equator is 0 degrees and at the poles it is 90 degrees. Because the Earth is spherically shaped, light striking the planet above the equator is spread over a wider region, causing the light to be less intense. As you intuitively knew, it is cooler in Nome, Alaska, than in Quito, Ecuador. The reason for this difference in temperature is latitude.

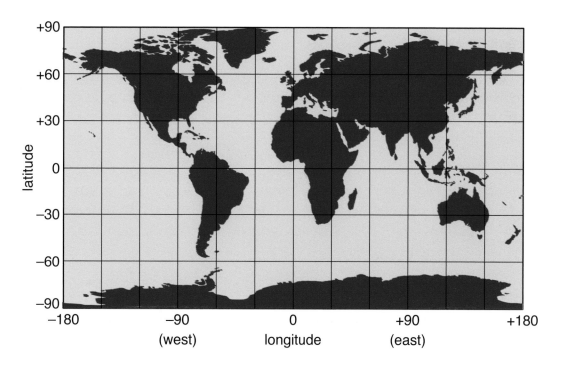

Figure 3

Want to Know More?

See appendix for Our Findings.

Further Reading

NASA News. "Measuring Solar Insolation." Available online. URL: http://Earthobservatory.nasa.gov/Newsroom/NewImages/images.php3?img_id=4803. Accessed October 5, 2008. This map shows how the amount of insolation varies across the Earth.

Russell, Randy. "Solar Radiation at Earth," April 2007. Available online. URL: http://www.windows.ucar.edu/tour/link=/earth/climate/sun_radiation_at_earth.html. Accessed October 5, 2008. Russell does a great job of explaining how latitude affects angle of insolation.

Texas State Energy Conservation Office. "Texas Renewable Energy Projects." Available online. URL: http://www.infinitepower.org/projects.htm. Accessed February 7, 2009. The conservation office of Texas provides a list of renewable energy projects in the state.

Scope and Sequence Chart

This chart aligns the experiments in this book with some of the National Science Content Standards. (These experiments do not address every national science standard.) Please refer to your local and state content standards for additional information. As always, adult supervision is recommended and discretion should be used in selecting experiments appropriate to each age group or to individual students.

Standard	Grades 5–8	Grades 9–12
Physical Science		
Properties and changes of properties in matter	1, 3, 5, 16, 18	1, 3, 5, 16, 18
Chemical reactions	7	7
Motions and forces		
Transfer of energy and interactions of energy and matter	1, 2, 6, 18, 19, 20	1, 2, 6, 18, 19, 20
Conservation of energy and increase in disorder		
Life Science		
Cells and structure and function in living systems		
Reproduction and heredity		
Regulation and behavior		

Populations and ecosystems	6, 7	6, 7
Diversity and adaptations of organisms		
Interdependence of organisms		
Matter, energy, and organization in living systems		
Biological evolution		
Earth Science		
Structure and energy in the Earth system	all	all
Geochemical cycles	3, 5, 6, 7, 14, 16	3, 5, 6, 7, 14, 16
Origin and evolution of the Earth system		
Origin and evolution of the universe		
Earth in the solar system	10	10
Nature of Science		
Science in history	2, 9, 15, 18	2, 9, 15, 18
Science as an endeavor	all	all

Grade Level

Setting

The experiments are classified by materials and equipment use as follows:

- Those under SCHOOL LABORATORY involve materials and equipment found only in science laboratories. Those under SCHOOL LABORATORY must be carried out there under supervision of the teacher or another adult.

- Those under HOME involve household or everyday materials. Some of these can be done at home, but call for supervision.

- The experiments classified under OUTDOORS may be done at the school or at the home, but call for supervision.

SCHOOL LABORATORY

1.   The Heat-Retaining Properties of Water and Soil

5.   Factors That Affect Evaporative Rates

6.   Sources of Carbon Dioxide in the Air

8.   Variables That Affect Cloud Formation

10.   How Does Distance Affect Solar Energy Absorption?

16.   How Much Dew Forms at Night?

18.   A Custom Temperature Scale

HOME

3.   How Are Snowflakes Formed?

4.   Modeling El Niño

9.   What Type of Hair Makes the Most Accurate Hygrometer?

11.   When Fronts Collide

12.   How Do Tornadoes Form?

14.   How Does Topography Affect Flash Flooding?

OUTDOORS

Our Findings

1. THE HEAT-RETAINING PROPERTIES OF WATER AND SOIL

Idea for class discussion: Show students a beaker of soil and a beaker of water. Explain that the class is going to do an experiment to find out which one retains heat longer. Ask students to make predictions about what their experiment will show. Revisit predictions after the activity.

Analysis

1. Answers will vary.
2. In a controlled experiment, all variables must be the same except the one being tested.
3. soil
4. water
5. Answers will vary.
6. Lake Michigan is able to retain heat longer than the air and soil around it.
7. The heat-retaining ability of water moderates temperatures around the coast.

2. STUDENT-CONSTRUCTED WEATHER STATIONS

Idea for class discussion: Find out how many students watch or read weather reports. Ask why they are interested in these reports and how they use them.

Analysis

1. Answers will vary, but should include a comparison of data from the constructed weather station and the weather stations used by meteorologists.
2. Answers will vary depending on student's weather observations.

128

3. Barometers measure atmospheric pressure, which changes when the weather changes. If the barometric pressure increases, it generally predicts warm, clear weather. If barometric pressure decreases, you can usually expect cooler temperatures and/or precipitation.

4. Wind occurs when there is a difference in air pressure. Wind blows from the direction of a high-pressure front toward the low-pressure front. The direction that the wind is blowing can tell the direction that weather patterns are moving and can also predict the onset of changing weather.

5. The uneven heating of Earth ultimately creates all weather patterns on this planet because air moves more rapidly when it is heated. Therefore, changes in temperature have a large impact on weather patterns. Warm temperatures increase air pressure and cause the air to move away from that location. When warm air and cool air meet, precipitation forms. For example, the rapid cooling of warm air creates thunderstorms.

6. Answers will vary but could include humidity, cloud patterns, altitude, and the location of bodies of water.

3. HOW ARE SNOWFLAKES FORMED?

Idea for class discussion: Have students work with partners to write a hypothesis explaining how snowflakes form. Have students review their hypotheses after the experiment.

Analysis

1. Student sketchs of ice crystals will vary.

2. Answers will vary. Students' crystals should have a shape similar to that of snowflakes, but they may not appear as flattened because they did not travel through the atmosphere.

3. The crystals formed on fishing line instead of in a cloud, and they did not pass through varying temperatures (the temperature just got steadily colder within the chamber). However, just as with real snowflakes, these crystals were formed by the condensation of water in very cold conditions, the ice took on similar shapes, and as snowflakes must form around a substrate such as dust, the man-made crystals formed on the fishing line.

4. Yes. The sponge is a source of water, which forms the water vapor necessary for condensation of ice crystals to occur. Snowflakes would not have formed without moisture.

5. Regular ice is frozen water and its temperature is about 0°C. In order for ice crystals to form, the temperature must be colder than the freezing point of water. Dry ice is solid carbon dioxide, which is much colder than ice made from water, so it enables the temperature within the chamber to be much colder.

6. Water cannot condense unless it has a substrate to condense onto. The substrate in the snow chamber is the fishing line. Ice crystals cannot simply form in thin air without some kind of particle to nucleate them (such as dust or bacteria).

4. MODELING EL NIÑO

Idea for class discussion: Find out how many students are familiar with El Niño. Explain the meaning of the term.

Analysis

1. The red oil shifts toward the "west" side, causing more blue water to be present in the "east" side. This represents normal conditions in the Pacific Ocean where the eastern Pacific contains a large amount of cool water created by upwelling and the western Pacific contains a lot of warm water.

2. The red oil moves back toward the "east," and the red and blue layers equalize. This represents the conditions during El Niño.

3. Clouds are condensed regions of water vapor. The water vapor that condenses into clouds had to evaporate from a body of water at some point. Water evaporates much faster from warm water than from cool water. Therefore, when water is warmer, as it is in the western Pacific during non-El Niño years, precipitation is formed in the western Pacific due to the evaporation of water there, and then is carried onto land by the westward-blowing trade winds.

4. wet weather in the areas near the eastern Pacific; dry conditions in landmasses west of the Pacific

5. Because El Niño causes the nutrient-rich cool water from deep in the Pacific to be pushed downward, there will be less food available to the fish and other marine life in the eastern Pacific. This causes fish to move into deeper water or farther away from land to find food, or they die. The movement of fish can therefore affect birds and other land animals that rely on fish as a food source.

5. FACTORS THAT AFFECT EVAPORATIVE RATES

Idea for class discussion: Have students work with partners to define evaporation and condensation. Briefly discuss the roles of these two processes in weather.

Analysis

1. Answers will vary depending on which factors were chosen. Answer should include an explanation why those factors were chosen.

2. Answers will vary depending on which factors were chosen and experimental results. High water temperature, wind movement, large surface area, and low humidity should all increase evaporation rates. The one that increases it the most depends on the experimental conditions.

3. Dry, windy conditions over a body of warm water would cause the highest rate of evaporation.

4. Answers will vary, but generally the most evaporation occurs over the ocean, then the clouds move over the land for precipitation to occur.

5. Explanations of the design of the controlled experiment will vary. Student answers should focus on the importance of having control factors in an experiment so that the experiment results are only based on the one factor that was changed, and nothing else.

6. SOURCES OF CARBON DIOXIDE IN THE AIR

Idea for class discussion: Help students relate the production of carbon dioxide to the natural process of cellular respiration as well as to fossil fuel combustion.

Analysis

1. Bar graphs will vary but should include labeled axes with four samples on the X-axis and number of ammonia drops on the Y-axis. Sample D should have the highest bar (near 60 drops), C will be next, followed by B, and then A (which should have zero drops).

2. The baking soda and vinegar sample should have the most because it is almost pure carbon dioxide. Atmospheric air should have the least. It most likely did not even affect the color of the test tube liquid.

3. Answers may vary, but will most likely be "yes," depending on lab results. Responses should include an explanation of why they answered as they did.

4. Answers will vary but may include use an alternate fuel source, a mechanism to convert carbon dioxide to another gas, etc.

5. Answers will vary. Some responses may include: burning of coal, industrial processes, deforestation, and agricultural development. Methods of decreasing emission will vary but may include using alternate fuel sources, planting more trees, and decreasing industrialization.

6. Answers will vary but may include carpooling, using public transportation, staying home more often, riding a bike instead of a car, etc.

7. LEVELS OF ULTRAVIOLET RADIATION IN LOCAL ECOSYSTEMS

Idea for class discussion: Ask students where they would expect to receive more ultraviolet radiation, in the forest or at the beach? Have students explain why. Relate their answers to the effects of UV radiation on organisms in ecosystems.

Analysis

1. Answers will vary depending on the ecosystem chosen. Answer should include an explanation of why they chose that particular location.

2. Answers will vary. Students should describe the parts of their experiment that remained the same between the two locations with the exception of the one factor that was being tested. This is important because in a controlled experiment, all variables should remain the same except for the one being tested so that the results will be based only on the one factor that was changed.

3. Answers will vary. Students should include a comparison of the UV levels in both of their chosen ecosystems.

4. The measured UV light could vary depending on altitude, cloud cover, tree cover, proximity to a major city, and the ground cover (water, snow, and sand reflect light, which would cause a higher reading).

5. Answers will vary depending on the organisms in the particular ecosystem chosen but may include damage to plants, algae, and plankton, which are at the base of the food web; damage to bacteria

and fungi, which are decomposers in the ecosystem; and increased skin damage and skin cancer in humans and animals.

6. Answers will vary but may include ecosystems in alpine regions because of higher elevation and reflection from snow; marine ecosystems near the equator because of increase in sunlight and reflection from the water; ecosystems in Antarctica, Australia, and New Zealand, because of the ozone hole.

8. VARIABLES THAT AFFECT CLOUD FORMATION

Idea for class discussion: Show the class a picture of cirrus clouds and a picture of cumulus clouds. Ask students to work in small groups to suggest some variables that affect the formations of clouds.

Analysis

1. Answers will vary depending on student results, but should include a sketch and a description of the cloud they created.

2. The ice caused the air at the top of the jar to become cooler so that when the warm air came in contact with it, the water vapor would condense into a cloud. Without ice, the air would not cool and a cloud would not form.

3. The match produced smoke, which contains tiny particles that act as condensation nuclei.

4. The boiling water chamber produced more of a cloud. Boiling water produces more water vapor contained in the air than tap water.

5. Most clouds form over the ocean because it is a very large body of water, so a great deal of evaporation can occur.

6. Answers will vary. Students should come up with a chamber that can be compressed to raise the pressure so that a cloud will form. One way to do this is by securing a balloon over the neck of the jar, then pressing in. The other factors of the experiment should remain basically the same as this test.

9. WHAT TYPE OF HAIR MAKES THE MOST ACCURATE HYGROMETER?

Idea for class discussion: Ask students if they can think of a natural fiber that always contracts when the weather is humid. Explain that hair has this ability.

Analysis

1. Answers will vary. Students should hypothesize which hair type will be more accurate and justify their answer.

2. The hydrogen bonds between keratin molecules can be disrupted by water molecules, causing a hair shaft to lengthen by about 2.5 percent in 100 percent humidity.

3. More humidity will cause the pointer to move downward because the hair becomes longer as the water molecules are absorbed.

4. Answers will vary depending on student results. Students should compare their results from each hygrometer to an amount measured using an electronic hygrometer or a local weather report.

5. Answers will vary based on student results. Since the hygrometers were calibrated, all types should have similar results, but the chemically treated hair will probably move the pointer more.

6. Answers will vary. Students should tell whether or not their hypothesis was justified, and if it was not, they should explain why.

7. Humidity levels change throughout the day depending on the temperature and the chance of precipitation. Hotter temperatures and the prospect of precipitation can cause the humidity level to increase.

10. HOW DOES DISTANCE AFFECT SOLAR ENERGY ABSORPTION?

Idea for class discussion: Tell students that there is a relationship between how much heat an object receives and the distance of that object from the source of heat. Ask for some speculation about that relationship. Explain that this is the topic of today's activity.

Analysis

1. Controlling factors is very important in any experiment in order to ensure that the results are due to the experimental factor and not any other factors.

2. Answers will vary. Students should describe the control factors that they used in their experiment such as measuring the same amount of soil in each cup and using the same type of sunlight bulb for each sample.

3. The soil sample placed closest to the sun lamp should have absorbed the most energy. This would be determined by measuring the temperature of the soil samples; the hottest one absorbed the most energy.

4. Soil that is closer to the sunlight will absorb more energy; soil that is farther away from sunlight absorbs less energy.

5. Answers will vary but may include the following: The energy from sunlight is reflected or absorbed by particles in the air as it travels toward the soil. Therefore, those samples that are closer to the lamp absorb more energy because less of it has been diffused. Soil samples that are farther away absorb less energy because more of it is diffused along the way.

6. Areas on the Earth that are closer to the Sun (higher elevation) and that receive more direct sunlight (near the equator) receive more energy from the Sun than those at lower elevations and at the poles.

11. WHEN FRONTS COLLIDE

Idea for class discussion: Show students a weather map and have them interpret it as fully as possible. Point out the fronts and explain that they are the topics of today's laboratory.

Analysis

1. Answers will vary. Students should hypothesize what will happen when the two types of water combine and justify their reasoning.

2. The red (warm) water moved on top of the blue (cold) water.

3. Warm water moves on top of the cold water because the molecules in the warm water are moving faster and are spread farther apart. This makes the warm water less dense than the cold water; therefore, it layers on top of the cold water.

4. Answers will vary based on student hypothesis in question 1. Students should explain why their hypothesis was not valid if their results proved it wrong.

5. It is similar to air masses mixing in the atmosphere because when fronts collide, warm air moves over top of cold air just as the warm water moves on top of the cold water. It is different in this case because it uses water instead of air; and the fronts met while moving at the exact same speed, so they simply layer on top of each other. In the atmosphere, the layering effect is determined by which front is approaching.

6. Answers will vary. Clouds are formed when fronts collide, so all types of precipitation and storms are created from the collision of two fronts. Answers may include rain, snow, thunderstorms, tornadoes, hurricanes, etc.

12. HOW DO TORNADOES FORM?

Idea for class discussion: Ask how many students have personal experience with tornadoes. Invite those students to tell what they remember about the event. If no student has experienced tornadoes, have them describe the images they have seen on the news.

Analysis

1. Students sketches will vary.

2. Students created a spiraling motion in the upper bottle that stretched down to the lower bottle. The "tornado" generally spirals and twists from side to side as the water empties out of the top bottle. When there is no water left in the top bottle, the tornado stops.

3. Swirling the bottles creates a spiraling vortex, much like the one created within a supercell by the merging of two different fronts. Without the spiral movement, water will just pass from the top bottle to the bottom one.

4. the spiraling force, created when the bottles were rotated, and the downward pull created when the water flows into the bottom bottle by the force of gravity

5. Answers will vary, but may include the following: The bottle tornado is similar in shape, rotation, and movement to a real tornado. Both tornadoes have a downward pull as well as a rotating force. However, the bottle tornado is contained in water, not air, and it does not cause widespread damage or move in a lateral direction.

6. Tornadoes have spiraling winds that create an upward draft surrounding a column of cool air being forced downward. Because of the variation in wind speed and direction, things tend to be whipped around quite a bit more than if a gust of wind blew in from one direction. Additionally, the rotation tends to pick up debris (as small as dust or as large as vehicles, rooftops, and mobile homes) and carry it some distance. The impact of debris held in a storm can cause as much if not more damage than the winds alone.

13. TEMPERATURE AND BAROMETRIC PRESSURE

Idea for class discussion: Ask students to define temperature and barometric pressure. Explain that this laboratory will help determine whether or not those two weather factors influence each other.

Analysis

1. Answers will vary. Students should create a hypothesis predicting the type of relationship that will be found between temperature and pressure and justify their reasoning.

2. In closed containers, such as tires, increasing the temperature increases the pressure because the particles move faster and collide with the container. This is not the case with atmospheric pressure, where the pressure decreases when the temperature rises. In winter, when temperatures are low, pressure in the tire will fall, thus drivers have to increase it.

3. For full credit, students should create a labeled scatter graph plotting the results from their experiment. All axes should be properly labeled and graph should include a title.

4. Answers will vary depending on student results, but most graphs should show a trend—as temperature increases, pressure decreases.

5. Answers may vary, but generally pressure decreases when temperature increases. Students should tell whether or not this trend agreed with their predictions.

6. Air pressure can be influenced by wind, weather developments (storms, etc.), and humidity.

7. The atmospheric pressure can be used to predict weather patterns because the barometer reading generally drops just before a storm, but rises when the storm is passing.

14. HOW DOES TOPOGRAPHY AFFECT FLASH FLOODING?

Idea for class discussion: Ask how many students have personal experience with a flash flood. Invite those students to share their experiences. If no student has experienced a flash flood, have them describe the images they have seen on the news.

Analysis

1. Answers will vary. Some answers may include, but are not limited to, elevation, amount of rainfall, type of soil, saturation of soil, number of trees in an area, depth of the river, and speed of the river.

2. Correct answer is "yes," but answers may vary based on student opinion, as long as the answer is justified. The shape and size of a

17. DOES SUNSET COLOR VARY WITH WEATHER CONDITIONS?

Idea for class discussion: Ask students to suggest some reasons for the almost universal love of sunsets.

Analysis

1. Answers will vary. Student hypotheses should state how they believe sky color is related to weather conditions.

2. The most dramatic colors generally appear just after the Sun recedes past the horizon.

3. Answers will vary based on weather conditions and student observations. Students should compare the colors of the sunset in the pictures that they took each day.

4. Answers may vary depending on actual weather conditions observed. Generally, the sunset will appear more red after a day of rain or high humidity. There will be more colors in the sky if there are more clouds present. The sunset will tend to be more blue and have fewer colors on dry days when there is little humidity.

5. Answers will vary depending on student hypothesis. Students should state whether or not their hypothesis was accurate and if it was not, they should explain why.

6. The color of a sunset is not only affected by humidity and cloud cover, but also by the amount of pollution, dust, and smoke in the air. Small particles in the air can cause reflection of light, causing the sunset to be more red.

18. A CUSTOM TEMPERATURE SCALE

Idea for class discussion: Ask students how they would monitor temperatures if they were on a deserted island.

Analysis

1. The liquid rose higher in the straw as the temperature rose.

2. Liquids expand when they are warmed, so the liquid takes up more volume than it did when it was cooler.

3. Adding alcohol to the water makes it expand faster when heated.

4. Answers will vary depending on student results. Students should compare their custom scale to readings in Celsius and Fahrenheit.

5. Students' readings of Celsius and Fahrenheit temperatures should agree with the given formula.

6. Answers will vary depending on students' custom scale. Student answers should include a calculated conversion factor to convert their scale to Celsius.

7. Answers will vary depending on students' custom scale. Student answers should include a calculated conversion factor to convert their scale to Fahrenheit.

19. A CONVECTION BOX

Idea for class discussion: Have two groups of students give their own definitions of convection. Write these on the board and revisit them after the experiment.

Analysis

1. the cyclic behavior of air rising and sinking due to differences in density

2. situation that occurs when warm air moves over cool air, trapping it

3. The smoke produced by burning paper towels made it possible to see the movement of air.

4. Smoke was pulled into the chimney. Inside the box, the smoke warmed and rose out of the other chimney.

5. The smoke was trapped on the bottom of the shoe box.

20. INTENSITY OF INSOLATION

Idea for class discussion: Ask students to explain why it is warmer in summer than in winter.

Analysis

1. 90 degree angle

2. 33 degree angle

3. 90 degree angle

4. 33 degree angle

5. Answers may vary. As the angle of insolation increases, temperature decreases.

Glossary

absolute zero   the point at which all molecule motion ceases, 0°Kelvin (°K)

air mass   large body of air with uniform characteristics such as temperature and moisture content

anemometer   device for measuring wind speed, usually calibrated in miles per hour

barometer   device for measuring air pressure, usually calibrated in inches of mercury or millibars

basal cell carcinoma   the most common form of skin cancer; originates from the lower or basal layer of skin; slow growing and not likely to spread

boiling point elevation   the rising of the normal boiling point of a liquid when another substance is added to the liquid

buoyant   able to float or rise toward the surface of a liquid

cataracts   condition of the eye in which the lens becomes cloudy, making it difficult to see

chlorofluorocarbons (CFCs)   group of chemicals once used as refrigerants and propellants in aerosol cans. In the atmosphere, CFCs damage the ozone layer.

circadian rhythms   changes in the body that occur every 24 hours

cold front   front edge of an advancing cold air mass

condensation   process of changing from a gaseous state to a liquid or solid state

condensation nuclei   particles in the atmosphere on which water molecules condense

convection   transfer of heat by the movement or circulation of molecules

convectional rain   rain produced when warm, moist air rises and cools

convection cell   a circular pattern or loop of rising and sinking air or water

convection currents   circular currents caused by a difference in temperature in upper and lower levels of a liquid or gas

coral bleaching   stress-induced loss of color in coral due to the release of symbiotic one-celled algae

cumulonimbus clouds   dense, vertical clouds that are also known as thunderheads

cyanobacteria   photosynthetic bacteria that serve as the base of many aquatic food chains

cyclonic rain   rain produced when two different air masses meet, and the warmer air is pushed upward, causing it to cool and the water vapor in it to condense

deforestation   removal of trees and other vegetation from Earth's surface

density   the mass of an object per unit volume

dew point   temperature at which water vapor in the air will condense at a specific pressure and humidity

diffract   to bend light into its different wavelengths

electromagnetic radiation   electric and magnetic waves that travel at the speed of light

electromagnetic spectrum   the full range of frequencies of electromagnetic radiation

El Niño   weather condition that leads to warming of the equatorial Pacific waters

El Niño-Southern Oscillation   an atmospheric-oceanic event that occurs irregularly because of changes in ocean temperatures

evaporation   process of changing from a liquid state to a gaseous state

firn   old, packed snow that has become dense from melting and refreezing

food chain   one path along which energy travels through an ecosystem

food web   all of the interconnecting paths along which energy may travel through an ecosystem

frost   frozen water formed when condensation occurs at temperatures below freezing

Fujita scale   system for ranking the severity of tornadoes on a scale ranging from F0 (mild) to F5 (severe) based on wind damage

global warming   an overall increase in Earth's temperature caused by the accumulation of gases in the atmosphere

greenhouse gases   atmospheric gases, primarily water vapor, methane, carbon dioxide, and ozone, that trap the Sun's heat near Earth's surface

guttation   excretion of water from the tips of plants at night

heat capacity   amount of heat required to raise the temperature of 1 gram (g) of a substance 1° Celsius (°C).

heat index   index that combines temperature and humidity to reflect how the air feels

humidity   amount of water vapor in the air

hydrogen bond   weak bond between the positively charged end of one molecule and the negatively charged end of another

hygrometer   instrument used to measure the amount of moisture in the air

hyperthermia   condition in which the body temperature is higher than normal

infrared energy   electromagnetic radiation whose wavelengths lie between those of red light and the shortest microwaves

insolation   solar radiation that strikes the Earth

jet stream   band of high-speed, upper-altitude winds that move in a westerly direction

keratin   strong fibrous protein found in skin, hair, and nails

La Niña   weather condition that leads to cooling of the equatorial water of the Pacific Ocean

levee   man-made embankment along a waterway that helps control the flow of water

lightning   discharge of static electricity between two clouds or between clouds and the ground

malignant melanoma   type of skin cancer that begins in the pigment-producing cells that is often fatal

melatonin   hormone produced by the pineal gland that affects natural daily rhythms

meteorologist   scientist who studies and forecasts the weather

methane   commonly known as natural gas, a simple compound that can be used as fuel

orographic rain   rain produced when moist air is forced over a tall land mass such as a mountain

osteoporosis   condition in which bones lose density and become more susceptible to fracture

ozone   compound made from three oxygen atoms that is a pollutant at ground level; in the upper atmosphere, ozone protects Earth from ultraviolet radiation

photosynthesis chemical reaction that occurs in organisms that contain chlorophyll in which the energy of light is used to convert water and carbon dioxide into glucose and oxygen

pineal gland gland in the brain that secretes melatonin

plankton drifting organisms such as tiny plants, animals, protists, and bacteria that float at the surface of the ocean

point of saturation point at which no more of a substance can be absorbed

polar molecule molecule having positively and negatively charged poles or ends

precipitation any form of water that falls to the Earth

rain gauge device that collects and measures rainfall

rain shadow effect the result of the process that leads to a dry region of land on the side of a mountain away from the wind

root pressure force that moves water up from the roots of a plant into stems and leaves

smog air pollutants formed when heat and light cause reactions between various chemicals such as ground-level ozone and carbon-based substances formed by the chemical union of two or more elements

squamous cell carcinoma type of cancer that develops in flattened cells that are found in skin and in the lining of many organs

supercell large, rotating, severe thunderstorm that can last for hours and may produce tornadoes

symbiotic relationship relationship between organisms of two different species that is beneficial to both organisms

temperature inversion atmospheric condition caused by the layering of warm air over cooler air, preventing the cooler air from rising

tornado violent, rotating windstorm, characterized by a funnel-shaped cloud, that occurs over land

tornado warning an alert from the National Weather Service that a tornado has been spotted and everyone should take cover

tornado watch an alert from the National Weather Service that weather conditions may produce a tornado

trade winds strong easterly winds that blow through the subtropics and the tropics

transpiration loss of water from plants through the small pores in leaves

ultraviolet light invisible part of the electromagnetic spectrum in which waves are shorter than visible light but longer than X-rays

upwelling upward movement of cold, nutrient-rich ocean water to the surface

UVA long wavelength ultraviolet radiation that can cause moderate skin damage

UVB medium wavelength ultraviolet radiation that causes mutations in DNA, leading to skin cancer and other serious conditions

UVC short wavelength, high energy ultraviolet radiation that does not reach Earth's surface

visible light spectrum the part of the electromagnetic spectrum that includes visible light

vitamin D vitamin made in the skin that is essential for bone formation

warm front front edge of an advancing warm air mass

water cycle circulation of Earth's water through the environment

wavelength distance between the crests of two adjacent waves

wind vane device that indicates the direction from which wind is blowing

Internet Resources

The World Wide Web is an invaluable source of information for students, teachers, and parents. The following list is intended to help you get started exploring educational sites that relate to the book. It is just a sample of the Web material that is available to you. All of these sites were accessible as of February 2009.

Educational Resources

AccuWeather.com. National Weather Maps, 2008. Available online. URL: http://www. accuweather.com/. Accessed December 26, 2008. National weather maps on this Web site show radar, satallite views, temperatures, and weather advisories.

Air Now. Local Forecasts and Conditions. Available online. URL: http://cfpub.epa. gov/airnow/index.cfm?action=airnow.local. Accessed October 10, 2008. On this government-backed site, you can select a state and access the recent air pollution information.

Calvert, James, B. "Introduction to Weather," October 1, 2008. Available online. URL: http://mysite.du.edu/~jcalvert/index.htm. Accessed October 9, 2008. Dr. Calvert, an associate professor emeritus of the University of Denver, provides information on many topics related to meteorology.

Intellcast.com, 2008. Available online. URL: http://www.intellicast.com/. Accessed December 26, 2008. The intellicast Web site provides a full-screen interactive U.S. weather map and global weather maps.

National Oceanic and Atmospheric Administration. Satellite and Information Service. Available online. URL: http://www.osei.noaa.gov/. Accessed October 13, 2008. This NOAA Web site shows current satellite images as well as snow cover, volcanic activity, dust storms, and other significant weather events.

National Oceanic and Atmospheric Administration. United States Interactive Climate Pages. Available online. URL: http://www.cdc.noaa.gov/data/usclimate/. Accessed February 7, 2009. On this Web site, one can click on a map of the United States to learn about a region's climate.

National Severe Storm Labs. "Severe Thunderstorm Climatology," August 29, 2003. Available online. URL: http://www.nssl.noaa.gov/hazard/. Accessed October 15, 2008. This Web page explains the science behind severe storms.

PBS Online. "El Niño," January 1998. Available online. URL: http://www.pbs.org/wgbh/nova/elniño/. Accessed October 15, 2008. This colorful Web site offers information on the anatomy of El Niño and explains how researchers gather information.

Unisys Weather. Available online. URL: http://weather.unisys.com/. Accessed October 15, 2008. Unisys provides a complete source of graphical information on weather as well as satellite images.

University of Michigan. U-M Weather, 2004. Available online. URL: http://cirrus.sprl.umich.edu/wxnet/. Accessed October 16, 2008. This Web site provides forecasts, weather cams, weather maps, and more.

University of Wisconsin. Interactive Climate Map. Available online. URL: http://www.uwsp.edu/geo/faculty/ritter/interactive_climate_map/climate_map.html. Accessed October 16, 2008. By clicking on the interactive map, a graph appears showing precipitation and temperature. Clicking on a city provides longitude, characterization of summer and winter weather, and photographs.

Weather.com. The Weather Channel, 2008. Available online. URL: http://www.weather.com/. Accessed December 26, 2008. Weather.com provides a national weather map and stories related to weather.

World Meteorological Organization. World Weather Information Sevice. Available online. URL: http://www. worldweather.org/. This Web site provides global weather information and forecasts in several languages.

Index

R

rain gauge 6, 7, 10, 11
rain shadow effect 47
root pressure 96

S

smog 41, 115
snowflake 14, 15, 18
squamous cell carcinoma 42
sunset 98-102
supercell 67, 70, 71
symbiotic relationship 42

T

temperature inversion 111, 113-115
temperature scale 104

tornado 65, 67-70
tornado warning 71
tornado watch 71
trade winds 24
transpiration 96

U

ultraviolet radiation 38, 39, 41, 42
upwelling 20, 22
UVA 39, 41
UVB 39, 41
UVC 39, 41

V

visible light spectrum 38, 102
vitamin D 59, 60

W

warm front 62, 64, 65
water cycle 26
wavelength 38
weather lore 102
weather station 6, 7, 10-12
wind vane 6, 8, 10, 11

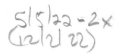